Japanese Antiques

Japanese Antiques

WITH A GUIDE TO SHOPS

By PATRICIA SALMON

AI PUBLISHERS

To my Japanese friends and associates who have contributed to this book far more than they know.

Published by Art International Publishers, 1-1-26 Azabudai, Minato-ku, Tokyo. Copyright in Japan, 1975, by Patricia Salmon. All rights reserved. Printed in Japan.
First printing, March, 1975
Second printing, October, 1975
Third printing, August, 1977
Book design and typography by Dana Levy

CONTENTS

FOREWORD

This book is an indispensable aid that is twenty years overdue. People have been buying Japanese antiques, often with taste but with little background information. Others are overwhelmed or intimidated by the amount of knowledge they feel necessary before buying Japanese art objects.

Such knowledge of course is not necessary; a good eye and a sound sense of what will decorate one's home and be enjoyable in daily life is sufficient. Yet some background on the history and culture of Japan and Japanese objects can do nothing but deepen one's pleasure with the things one buys. Naturally such knowledge will also directly affect one's taste and understanding and will provide a basis for new adventures in understanding.

This handy reference provides insights and information to open horizons in the world of Japanese antiques for both the experienced collector and the novice. Ms. Salmon's concise and delightful book is more than a service to the lover of beautiful Oriental things.

DAVID KIDD

Ashiya, 1974

THE JOY OF COLLECTING

If you have ever found yourself in a junk, second-hand, furniture, or antique shop; spotted an object whose shape, design, craftsmanship, or whatever, seemed to speak to you directly; taken it home and displayed it prominently to find that other people also found it appealing and wanted to know more about it or where you found it—if so, you have undoubtedly been bitten by the antiqueing bug. In fact, that is one of the reasons you happen to be reading this book.

The joy of collecting is for everyone. Do not let a lack of knowledge stop you or unsympathetic companions who have yet to be bitten intimidate you. Charge right in and enjoy every moment!

Collecting is a three-fold adventure. First of all there is the object itself that brings you pleasure. It may be a picture that interests you and gives you a sense of warm satisfaction each time you view it; a piece of woodwork that reflects in an instant the weeks, months, and perhaps years of work that went into its exquisite craftsmanship; or perhaps a piece of porcelain that "tings" like a bell when you thump it and is a joy to use filled with flowers or food or rather is just to be admired for its own special shape, colors, hand-painted scene, or sense of history. It is fun to speculate its former use and consider the owner who must have appreciated the object several decades, centuries, or millennia before you.

This leads to the second adventure of collecting, the pleasure that comes with learning more of the history and culture associated with an object. New doors open, and great vistas unfold, whether your taste in objects is specialized or eclectic. One culture may catch your fancy, but you cannot help also being confronted with the cross-pollination that was taking place centuries ago between various far-flung peoples and continents. If you happen to have a healthy curiosity —and who does not—this phase of collecting is deadly: it may lead you from a hobby into a profession, but it will always provide never-ending and fascinating adventures.

The third joy of collecting is the knowledge that usually the antique you buy today will have a greater monetary value tomorrow. Of course most collectors do not begin with the thought of making money, but, in the course of the game, tastes do change and eventually you find that you are willing to part with something purchased in the early stages of your collecting in order to add another antique that is more appealing to you at present. The more one haunts the antique shops, visits museums, and reads and learns about antiques, the more the appetite and taste develop, and eventually one desires and demands higher quality in his or her purchases. This also means higher prices. Many times, the growth of a collection can be largely financed from trading or selling previous purchases. Of course there are some items dear to the heart of each collector that never lose their original appeal, and these become the core, the personal note in any collection.

It is always wiser to look at an antique first from the point of view of its personal appeal to you. If it happens to have an investment value, good—but the object's primary reason for being in your possession is that it speaks to you. However, many people today are using art and antiques as an investment market. Such investors should treat antiques in a businesslike way. A serious businessman certainly would not commit monies to stocks and bonds without knowing and understanding something about the market, and for this purpose he studies, observes, and retains a well-qualified broker. The same should apply to antiques—study, train your eyes, and rely on the advice of a trusted, well-informed dealer.

However, for most the investment is a minor part of the incentive to collect and is only gratifying in that the objects we take pleasure in purchasing and living with can be counted on to appreciate in value rather than depreciate, which cannot be said for most of the other tangibles in our lives.

My first years in Japan were busy ones, occupied with beginning and maintaining a business. However, after the first year in residence, my spare time came to be devoted to exploring the antique shops in search of small curiosities that could be given as Christmas gifts. This search soon expanded into collecting beautiful objects that I wanted to be able to live with and enjoy, and eventually I began to study seriously, a pursuit I trust shall continue for many more fascinating years. Pleasurable hours were spent fondling objects unfamiliar to me and asking questions about them, their use, and what the people were like who made and enjoyed them. Talk with six dealers and you will average about four different stories (or maybe twelve), but eventually there will be some kind of consensus, and the pieces of the puzzle will fit.

My weekly column in a Tokyo English-language newspaper, *The Mainichi Daily News*, began in January 1972. Called "Antiqueing" the purpose of the column was to aid the beginning collector by giving a brief history of the object pictured, trace its development and use, and give suggestions for modern usage. This information was what I was seeking every time I managed to corner and could communicate with a knowledgeable shop owner. From this concept came this book.

Surprisingly, the most difficult objects to learn anything about were those used in daily living. They were so common that no one bothered to write about them, and few could remember where they originated or how they were used in past centuries.

In writing this book, I have at every turn consulted as many references as were available in English on the subjects covered, and when I could not find sufficient material, I consulted friends and experts. To those friends and acquaintances who have so generously given of their time and knowledge I owe a great debt of thanks, and indeed this book could not have come to print without them. For any errors, or differences of opinion that might occur, I take full responsibility.

I sincerely hope that this small book will be helpful in providing the beginning collector with some basic information, facts, and pointers on Japanese and Korean antiquities, and that the joy of collecting and adventure of learning will be as pleasurable and rewarding for the reader as they have been for me.

ACKNOWLEDGEMENTS

I would like to express my deep appreciation to Mr. David Kidd and Y. Morimoto of Ashiya, Japan, whose home and collection of Far Eastern antiques first sparked my serious interest in this field. Their constant friendship and guidance over a period of these several years have provided me not only with a great deal of information, but perhaps even more important, they instilled within me the incentive to search out many answers for myself and taught me to approach each object with an open and inquiring mind.

To Alice Boney, of New York and Tokyo, I also owe a debt of gratitude, for her time, patience, and encouragement given in helping a novice begin on a long but exhilarating road to learning.

To Mr. Yasuhiko Mayuyama, who has offered not only advice but has taken precious time from his busy schedule to read the manuscript and suggest alterations, I can only say a thousand thanks.

To Taku Seguchi, a lacquer artisan of Kyoto, Mr. M. Matsushita, a Tokyo specialist in woodblock prints, and Messrs. Watanabe and Ando at Odawara Shoten, among many others too numerous to mention here, I would like to convey my heartfelt thanks for the time they have so willingly spent discussing the history of certain objects with me or researching certain points.

I am indebted to Mrs. Julie Cohen for her constant cooperation in providing antiques for photographs and for her helpful insights.

To all shopkeepers I convey my gratitude for being there when I visited their shops and for responding to my questions and enthusiasms.

I would also like to take this opportunity to say a special thank you to those who have been kind enough to lend their pictures for publication in this book. Each has been noted in the Photo Credits.

But for all of you, this book could not have come to print.

Patricia Salmon

Tokyo, 1974

COSMETIC BOXES—TEBAKO, KESHOBAKO

LACQUERED BOXES called *tebako* (literally, "hand box"), and *keshobako* (cosmetic box), came into vogue in Japan during the tenth and eleventh centuries. Women of the aristocracy used these boxes to store their mirrors, combs, scissors, and toilet accessories such as powder, tooth black, incense, and rouge pots. *Tebako* were also sometimes used for stationery and private papers.

To accommodate so much, the casket-shaped *tebako* were quite large—usually around ten inches wide. Originally most of them contained smaller lacquered boxes, all decorated in harmony with the larger container in patterns inspired by nature. Grasses, flowers, insects, and birds were a few favored subjects. Unfortunately, most of these smaller containers have, over the years, become separated and lost from the parent box.

The oldest known *tebako* dates from late in the Heian period (794—1185). It is a box of gold lacquer and mother-of-pearl inlay with a graceful design of wheels floating in a rippling stream. This traditional motif (also found on mirror backs of the same period) originated from the practice of floating wooden wheels in water to prevent them from drying out. This pattern was to appear frequently on lacquer objects during the following centuries.

Gold and black lacquer *tebako* may still be found on the antique market today, but the gold lacquer ones are expensive collectors' items. Black lacquer cosmetic boxes—usually decorated with gold flowers, butterflies, crests—can occasionally be found at a somewhat lesser price and make wonderful cosmetic kits, just as they were originally intended.

Brass rings or copper are found on two sides, attached to the boxes by discs of intricately worked metal. Woven cords in vibrant colors were originally slipped through the rings and tied on top of the box, although the cords are mostly missing today. Many have a shallow tray that is ideal for holding small items—brushes, tweezers, puffs—and the deep space below can be used for makeup bottles and jars.

Cosmetic box. Black lacquer on wood with gold *maki-e* fan design. Late sixteenth century. H. 3.5 in., L. 6.25 in.

COSMETIC STANDS—KYODAI

COSMETIC STANDS with drawers and a mirror rack on top, *kyodai*, came into popularity among the gentry during the late Muromachi and Momoyama periods (16th century). Prior to that time the casket-shaped *tebako* was used to hold toiletries.

Cosmetics, such as powder and natural vegetable and camellia oil pomade, were known to be used in the Orient by the ancient Chinese about 1500 B.C. As fashion changed with each successive period, so did makeup styles and the design of cosmetic containers.

Toward the end of the Chou dynasty, a rather flamboyant period from 1027—256 B.C., small round boxes of lacquer painted with sophisticated designs served as cosmetic containers. Often they were made in a nest of two or more with a comb to match. In the following Han dynasty, as the popularity of cosmetics grew, their containers became even more elaborate—hexagonal and flower shapes were introduced.

By the ninth century A.D., the cosmetic market (limited to the aristocracy) was booming in China. It was the end of the T'ang dynasty, and the vogue was for Chinese ladies to cover their forehead and cheeks with large dots of rouge made from the juice of crushed safflower petals. Meanwhile Chinese traders had begun to export their cosmetics and perfumes to Japan.

The Heian era in ninth century Japan was a time of great pomp and ceremony. In keeping with the rigid code of court conduct, members of the nobility wore twelve-layer kimonos and applied facial makeup according to a strict set of rules.

From the age of puberty, the lovely Heian lady was obliged to use black tooth dye, a concoction of iron shavings in vinegar mixed with powdered gallnuts. Facial hair was regarded as undesirable, so eyebrows were shaved and paint applied well above the browline. This paint, called *mayuzumi,* was a mixture of lamp soot and sesame oil.

For cleansing their skin, these gentle ladies used little cotton bags containing rice bran. It was said that to maintain gleaming black hair one should wash it with a special type of seaweed and then rinse it with warm water.

White face powder was introduced to Japan from China and Korea and made from white lead and chalk. In modern times it was banned because of its dangerous lead content.

The favored beauty treatment, still available in some drugstores (and of course pet stores) today, was an application of *uguisu no fun*, Japanese nightingale droppings.

Though most makeup ingredients have changed considerably since then, cosmetic boxes and stands can still be enjoyed as they were originally. The smaller containers are also ideal for sewing accessories, paper clips, and stamps.

Cosmetic stand. Black lacquer on wood with gold *maki-e* floral crest design. Mid eighteenth century. H. 25.5 in.

FANS—OGI, SENSU

THE GENERIC TERM for fan in Japanese is *ogi*, derived from *aogu*, "to cause a breeze." *Hi-ogi*, slat-fans, and their descendents are said to have evolved from the emperor's *shaku* ("sceptor"). Both are the same size and shape and are made of cypress, but the *shaku* is a solid piece of wood (it is also sometimes made of jade or ivory), whereas the *hi-ogi* is cut into thin strips and tied together by a cord.

According to legends, the *hi-ogi* came into being late in the Heian period, when the *shaku*, used exclusively by the emperor, was split into slats to hold memos regarding court ritual and protocol. Before long the *hi-ogi* became a favorite object for displaying art, and soon the emperor adopted the custom of presenting these special fans to members of the imperial family and the court. Never were they used as breeze makers. Rather, they were decorative, symbolic ornaments carried at certain court ceremonies by both men and women.

The *tessen* ("iron folding fan") is a variation of the slat fan. These sword-quality steel fans were used by the samurai. They were always decorated with the sun or moon and were considered an integral part of the battle costume.

There is a famous tale about a renowned sixteenth century general, who was summoned before the shogun for a suspected misdeed. The temper of the shogun was reputed to be so violent that he did not hesitate to slam the sliding doors on the heads of politely bowing subjects who had displeased him. The general, aware of this, laid his *tessen* on the doorsill, and when the shogun flew into a fury, the iron fan received the blow intended for his neck.

The traditional *sensu*, or paper fan, is still widely used in Japan today though few accounts regarding its origin have survived. Some historians speculate that its construction was suggested by the wing of a bat. In early days the paper fan was appropriately called *kōmori*, which means bat.

Through the centuries there has been a fan for every activity and occasion—a bewildering assortment.

There are special fans for the Noh drama, classical dances, the marriage ceremony, a maternity ceremony, ground breaking for a house or building, and even for reaching the age of seventy-seven! It seems that fans and Japanese cultural events have been inseparable for ten centuries.

Anyone living in Japan through one of its brief but hot summers can attest to the fact that fans have an indispensable modern use. Most interesting are the old ones, inexpensive and obtainable simply by rummaging in antique stores. If a beautiful painted one is discovered, it can be mounted as a wall hanging. Fan "paintings" are especially effective when hung in small areas—an entryhall or a dressing room.

Fan painting, by Korin (1658–1716). Colors on paper. Seventeenth century. 5.5 × 4.2 in.

GOLD LACQUER OBJECTS—MAKI-E

THE ART OF *maki-e* (gold and silver lacquer) as we now use the term was begun in the eighth century, at the end of the Nara period. Although indigenous to Japan as a technique, early *maki-e* retained a T'ang Chinese influence in design.

Maki-e is achieved by spreading and scattering gold or silver dust, flakes, nuggets, and leaf on a drawing done in sticky lacquer, which is applied over the hardened lacquer foundation.

Lacquer craft flowered during the late Heian period (794–1185), and gold and silver *maki-e* objects were exported to both China and Korea. The designs became more pictorial and simple at this time due to the progress made in the technique. The gold and silver powder used became finer in texture, and variations in color and the thickness of application gave even greater variety in the effects achieved. Inlaid mother-of-pearl was also used extensively together with the *maki-e*.

Pictorial treatment or realism in this lacquer "painting" began at this time. This purely Japanese expression continued in later eras to be an outstanding quality of the *maki-e* technique, which developed to great heights.

Since ancient days, lacquerers have been divided into two classes, the *nurimono-shi*, who work on the groundwork and foundation coats and the *maki-e-shi*, or gold lacquer masters, who do the decoration.

A few of the maki-e techniques that can be easily recognized in fine lacquer goods are *kin-maki-e* or *gin-maki-e* (gold or silver leaf), *nashiji* (widely scattered dust or flakes), *hirame* (small flakes of gold or silver placed irregularly on a colored surface), and *kirikane* (cut gold laid into the pattern, especially on banks of streams, tree trunks and bird feathers). *Takamaki-e* is decoration in low relief, while *hiramaki-e* is a design generally flush with the surface. Fine lacquer has always been highly appreciated in Japan and many parts of Europe, and currently there is a worldwide renaissance of regard for fine lacquer.

One to three weeks are necessary for each coat of lacquer to dry, and the number of coats can run into the hundreds. When one realizes the time, work, and skill that are required for fine lacquer, it is easy to feel a continuous sense of joy and appreciation in the ownership and use of lacquer objects.

Box for personal articles. Black lacquer on wood with fine gold *maki-e* flower design. Fifteenth century. H. 2.7 in., W. 4.8 in.

KIMONO TRAYS AND BOXES—MIDARÉ BAKO

THE LOVELY AND GRACEFUL Japanese kimono has long been the traditional costume for both men and women. The word itself means
clothing.

In the fashionable Edo period (1614–1868), people of all classes—
the wives of the warriors, gentry, and the wealthy merchant class—all
vied for top honors in being elegantly attired for every special occasion. Modern styles in kimono date from this era.

The arts were flourishing, and kabuki, which had a considerable
influence on woodblock prints of the day, also affected textile patterns.
The Genroku era (1688–1704) was known as a "golden age" for
kimonos, and no effort was considered too great in the design and
execution of the gorgeous fabrics. Many hours were spent by cultured
ladies discussing suitable motifs and colors with top designers of the
day. The results were breathtaking textile works of art.

Two major clothing changes were decreed each year. On the days
called *koromogae* ("changing of clothes"), heavier apparel was folded
away and lighter garments brought forth, or vice versa. The dates fall
on October 1 and June 1, and regardless of the sometimes inappro-
priate weather, even today there is always a change in attire.

Kimono fabrics, colors, and patterns are chosen in accord with
seasonal motifs, the age of the wearer, and the occasion.

For attending weddings, the long-sleeved, colorful *furisode* is worn
by young, unmarried women, while a black *tomesode* with a design
around the lower half of the skirt is suitable for married ladies. For
mourning, the black kimono with five white crests is traditional.

To store these lovely garments, trays or boxes made of lacquered
wood were used. Specially lacquered baskets or combinations of
basketry and lacquer were also popular. Often the lacquer was decorated in delicate gold patterns.

Japan's modern industrial boom has forced the kimono into a
luxury class that few can afford. Therefore, discarded kimono trays or
boxes, *midaré-bako*, can sometimes be found in antique shops. They
make beautiful, useful storage units or can be used as side tables on a
folding stand. In a guest room they are ideal as a tray for unpacked
accessories.

Kimono tray. Woven, lacquered bamboo with black lacquer rim decorated in gold *maki-e* floral pattern. Late nineteenth century. W. 15 in., L. 28 in.

NETSUKE

Netsuke are miniature works of art—carvings in wood, lacquer, ivory, metal, porcelain—which served as toggles for money purses, cases or bags containing such everyday necessities as flint and steel for striking a fire, tobacco, seals, and medicine.

Netsuke were part of Japanese attire from early in the Edo period (about 1600) until the twentieth century, when Western dress replaced the pocketless man's kimono. Their use has traditionally been a male prerogative. A Japanese lady always used the wide folds of her *obi* or the bottom of her kimono's long sleeve to carry accessories. But, a gentleman's costume was not complete without an attractive *netsuke*.

For utilitarian reasons *netsuke* had to meet certain requirements. The average *netsuke* was small, about 1 1/2 inches long. It had to be strong enough to support the pouch or case to which it was attached and to endure daily wear. Since it was handled and visible from all sides, the *netsuke* was finished all around and had two unobtrusive holes that would allow it to hang evenly on its cord. Its surface was smooth, with no appendages that might break off or tear a kimono sleeve.

The subject matter of *netsuke*, on the other hand, was free from restrictions. Craftsmen who carved them were not under the patronage of a daimyo nor did they belong to schools as did most other traditional Japanese artists. *Netsuke*, usually unsigned, were the work of individual craftsmen who imparted a unique personality and charm to each piece. Legends, ghost stories, animals (real and imaginary), genre scenes are just some of the innumerable themes depicted on *netsuke*. The amazing perfection of detail on such small objects is what makes them such exquisite works of art.

The first half of the nineteenth century is considered the golden age of *netsuke*. The tobacco pouch was at the height of its popularity, and many sculptors and other craftsmen—lacquerers, potters, metal artists—made *netsuke* as a sideline.

In Japan *netsuke* were everyday objects, not art objects. It was in Europe that they first caught the attention of collectors. Today *netsuke* enjoy an international reputation among antique and art connoisseurs. Not only are they fascinating little gems of sculpture, but they have substantial monetary value as well.

Netsuke, unsigned. Grazing horse in stag antler. Probably eighteenth century. H. 3 in.

Netsuke, signed Gechu. *Shishi* (lion) in ivory. Eighteenth century. H. 2.3 in.

PILLOWS—MAKURA

In ANCIENT JAPAN, pillows, *makura*, were made of straw or solid blocks of wood.

In China, around the time of the T'ang dynasty (618–907), porcelain pillows came into use, especially during the hot summers, since they remained cool throughout the night.

There were also pillow-boxes, or *hako-makura*, which originated with traveling nobles. The boxes of fine leather or pigskin covered with lacquer doubled as safes. They were used as pillows in inns along the way to ensure against robbery of money and valuables. Both types were later imported into Japan.

Pillows were probably the prerogative of Japanese men in early days. Prior to the Edo period (1614–1868), men wore their hair tied up or knotted in some form, while women wore theirs loosely flowing down their backs. This was mainly a practical arrangement, as the men were actively engaged in either work or warfare, while the women (of court circles) led quiet, sheltered lives.

Common ladies twisted or plaited their hair into simple forms and pinned it up out of the way of their manual labors.

During the civil wars in the Kamakura and Muromachi periods, the samurai had to wear their heavy steel helmets often. From the need for ventilation came the custom of shaving the forelock, with the remaining hair gathered into a chignon or topknot at the back of the head. This samurai fashion soon spread to the common people and endured for several centuries, until the end of the Edo period.

At the same time both men's and women's hair styles developed into many new and intricate shapes. Artisans especially trained in hairdressing arose, and a cosmetic paste of fat perfumed with aloes wood helped to mound the hair into rigid forms and hold it there for days. With these elaborate hairstyles, it would have been uncomfortable and messy to lay the head directly on bedding, and thus wooden and porcelain pillows came into widespread use.

Pillow boxes, many in lacquered woods with a small cylindrical padded cushion on top and tiny drawers for toilet accessories in the base, became very popular among ladies. Elaborately fashioned perfume pillows came into vogue among the gentry. The hollow lacquer pillow-box was carved into openwork designs, and an incense burner with perfumed wood was placed on the inside. Any lady sleeping on this ingenious pillow would wake with delicately fragrant tresses the next morning.

Porcelain and lacquer pillows make striking bolsters for a sofa or may be used as footrests or door stops.

Set of pillows. Black lacquer on wood with colored and gold *maki-e* decoration; silk cushion. Late nineteenth century. H. 4 in., L. 9.5 in.

PORTABLE MEDICINE BOXES—INRO

AN INRO IS A MEDICINE BOX that was carried as a personal accessory. *Inro* appeared in Japan during the late fifteenth century, when small four-tiered boxes about four inches square were imported from China. These boxes served as household containers for seals and thus acquired their name: *in* means seal or stamp; *ro*, vessel.

Through use, *inro* became convenient containers for medicine and, around the latter half of the sixteenth century, became portable. A bead called an *ojime*, "string fastener," was used to adjust the length of the cord that held the nested containers of the *inro* together. The *inro* swung from this cord, which looped over the *obi* and ended in a toggle called a *netsuke*.

Inro were first finished in plain black lacquer but later became embellished with gold lacquer, shell inlay, and other lavish decoration. It staggers the imagination to think of the enormous amount of time and work that went into these small, utilitarian objects.

The wooden core was so carefully prepared that even the thickness of numerous lacquer coats was considered. The tiered boxes had to fit snugly and be airtight. Up to sixty separate coats of lacquer might be applied to the core alone, with a drying time of up to one month between some coats.

When the coated core was finished, a special lacquer artist would apply the decoration. This ornamentation became so specialized that hundreds of techniques were invented—encrustation and inlay with tortoise shell, ivory, coral, wool, porcelain, and semiprecious stones and precious metals; painted lacquer; carved lacquer; and gold and silver sprinkled lacquer, among many others.

Inro enjoyed great popularity during the Edo period (1614–1868) and were prized objects of everyday use, mainly for men. They were admired, collected, and traded among the aristocracy and rich merchants. Their use continued until the advent of Western dress in Japan, around the middle of the nineteenth century.

Today *inro* are scarce and very expensive. They make handsome display pieces and, more importantly, represent an art form unique to old Japan.

Inro, signed Tachibana Gyokuzan. Black lacquer on wood with crawfish carved in red lacquer. Ivory *netsuke* carved with peony, plum, and chrysanthemum. Late eighteenth or early nineteenth century. H. 3.25 in.

CUP-WASHING STANDS AND BOWLS—HAISEN

Cup-washing stands or bowls, *haisen*, are used in the ritual of sharing saké.

At Japanese banquets or parties, one important feature is the exchange of saké drinking cups, *sakazuki*, between the host and his guests. At an informal party this exchange sometimes knows no bounds, with all present toasting and exchanging cups with great enthusiasm. If a particular geisha is appreciated, she will be offered a cup of saké by the gentleman she is attending, or for that matter, from a gentleman across the room.

The host first asks for the guest's cup and toasts him. The cup is then returned to the guest who returns the compliment by drinking to his host. During these exchanges, the cup is rinsed in water held in a special cup-washing container placed in the center of the table. One type of container is made of lacquer decorated with festive motifs. It has a removable metal cup in the center to hold the water. Another type is a large porcelain bowl, sometimes with a stem base.

The etiquette of sharing saké began centuries ago at parties where saké was served in a large cup that was shared by all. In those days men and women gathered on special days to share their food and wine, and this party was called a *sakamori, moru* meaning "to share." This custom is still practiced today in some places on the island of Kyushu.

Shrine festivals are always a reason for a saké drinking party. After the harvesting of the shrine rice, in which all members of the village take part, the community gathers to drink saké.

The small cup used for saké drinking today is called a *choko*. It has been in use for about two hundred years. Its introduction seems to have come when heating saké became popular. Originally the drink was served cold, in wooden containers. When saké of inferior quality came to be heated to improve its taste, the custom soon spread to all grades, and the porcelain cup helped to keep it warm.

Cup washing stands or bowls make attractive containers for food or canapés for parties. Fruit is especially attractive piled inside, and they are useful for a pretty plant or flower arrangement.

Saké cup washing stand. Blue-and-white porcelain, inside **border** with colored enamel decoration. Late nineteenth century. H. 3.5 in., D. 6 in.

INCENSE BOXES—KOBAKO

INCENSE BOXES, *kobako*, are containers made of lacquered wood or porcelain used for holding powdered or chipped incense.

Incense has been associated with religion since earliest recorded history. The Egyptians (circa 2500 B.C.) imported trees with aromatic resins from the Arabian and Somali coasts. Grains of resin mixed with spices were sprinkled on charcoal as a fragrant tribute to the great unfathomed powers.

In China's Han dynasty (206 B.C.–220 A.D.), the hill-shaped censer or burner was used by the royal household, and in later generations the burning of incense came into popular use as tribute to Chinese household gods and for ancestral prayers.

In Japan, incense is associated with both religion and culture. It was first imported into the country from India via China and became an important part of the Buddhist ritual. It was also assimilated into the native Shintoism.

The Shosoin Imperial Treasurehouse lists five small silk pouches used to contain incense and nine bags of *ebiko*, a blend of incenses used for scenting clothes. These entered the storehouse in 768 A.D. There is also a log of incense wood, *o-jukko*, from which the emperor cut one piece to be given to Shogun Ashikaga Yoshimasa in the mid fifteenth century.

It was Yoshimasa, a patron of the fine arts, who developed incense appreciation, *Kodo*, into an aesthetic cult in Japan. A game, *ko-awase*, was played in which various incenses would be tested and the guests would try to name the incense and describe its qualities, such as its "character," "color," or "taste." The refined sense of smell developed by incense was believed to cultivate the same mental tranquillity and physical poise as did the tea ceremony and flower arranging.

Incense also became an important part of the tea ceremony, used to create an atmosphere of peace and harmony in the tearoom. The incense burner, like the hanging scrolls, was chosen to harmonize with the setting and was to be admired by each guest. Sometimes a censer tea was performed. In this the incense burner and box were passed around, and each guest took a piece of incense and burned it, quietly enjoying the aroma.

Incense boxes were an important part of these cultural rituals, and great effort was put into their artistry and design. Highly intricate and refined patterns and techniques were used to produce these small works of art.

Incense box with inner trays. Black lacquer on wood decorated in colored and gold *maki-e* with mother-of-pearl inlay. Early nineteenth century. D. 9 in.

Incense box. Carved red lacquer on wood. Early seventeenth century. H. 2 in., L. 3.5 in.

SAKÉ CUP STANDS—HAI-DAI

SAKÉ CUP STANDS, *hai-dai*, first came into use during the Muromachi period (1333–1573). Plain wooden types were used in temples and shrines to offer saké to gods. In the mansions of the samurai and imperial court circles, lacquered stands were used to lift the small saké cups off the tatami floor and present them in a polite and gracious way to the lords and their retinue. Black lacquer, often exquisitely decorated in gold floral motifs, was in daily use, while red lacquer was used for special festive occasions such as the New Year's celebration and at weddings.

From the beginning of recorded history in China, wine or spirits were known to be served at all solemn feasts. Horns, gourds, and cups carved of precious stones or cast in bronze were used to drink the wine, and it was stored for fermentation in earthenware bottles. The wine was extracted from rice, and it is this same saké that is still being made today in Japan.

It was during the colorful Edo period (circa 1700) that porcelain saké cups first appeared, probably due to the new trend of heating the heady wine. This originated from the common classes, who found that saké of poor quality improved in taste when warmed. The hot liquid also helped keep them warm on cold winter nights.

This custom of heating saké soon became popular among all classes, and as a further adjunct to serving it in a pleasing manner, the merchants and commoners copied the accessories of the nobility and produced a porcelain stand, or the *hai-dai*, to hold the tiny cup.

Old cup stands remain in plentiful supply in Japan today and are still used, especially on festive occasions and at New Year's. The ones of porcelain are generally square in shape and decorated in colored enamels with a hole in the center for the saké cup. The lacquer cup stands are usually taller stands in round pedestal or square shapes, with a small round raised socket in the center for the cup. Both types make excellent candle holders, and the ones of porcelain may hold miniature bouquets for table settings or be used as ash trays.

Saké cup stands. Blue-and-white porcelain. Early nineteenth century. H. 1.7 in., 2 in.

Saké cup and stand: Cobalt blue porcelain; saké cup, white porcelain with colored enamel decoration. Early twentieth century. H. 3 in.

SHELL GAME LACQUER BOXES—KAI-OKE

KAI-OKE ARE HANDSOME LACQUERED CONTAINERS in hexagonal, octagonal, or round shapes that were used to store the shells of *kai-awase*, the "shell matching game." This was a popular parlor game in Japan from ancient times. Written records of this amusement date from the Heian era (794–1185), and it continued to be played until the end of the Edo period (1868).

The shells of a species of clam called *hamaguri* were used, since they have the unique characteristic that none other than the original pair will fit together. Initially, 360 half-shells were divided between two groups of players. Each side put forth one shell, and when the opposing player found a shell to match his, he won that shell.

The shells came to be beautifully painted or lacquered, and many innovations were introduced into this pastime. One delightful variation was the *uta-kai*, or "shell poem," game. One half of a poem was written in one shell and the other half in its mate. The successful player was required to be well read and witty, and it was not unusual for the poetry to allude to the manners and morals of court life, which were usually quite lively.

The Meiji Restoration brought modern industrialization, and the old leisure pursuits were soon traded for more expedient forms of entertainment. Western playing cards, introduced by the Portuguese in the sixteenth century, became popular, and elements of the old shell game were combined with the cards to form a new game. It is called *hana-awase*, or flower card game, and is still popular today.

The delicately painted shells of the discarded shell game are lovely as decorative pieces. The handsome lacquer boxes, the *kai-oke*, have ample room for storage. Many are decorated in gold lacquer designs, some retain their original heavy silk cords, and most have finely etched or engraved metalwork. Their graceful proportions echo an era when there was both time to create such objects of beauty and leisure to pursue the pleasure of their use.

Shell game boxes. Black lacquer on wood with etched metal fittings. Mid nineteenth century. H. 17 in.

CHOPSTICK HOLDERS, BOXES—HASHITATE, HASHIBAKO

THE CHOPSTICK HOLDER, *hashitate*, is such a common object that its origin is obscure. Most likely the first were a joint of bamboo or a wooden container used to hold these implements of eating. Until recently, a long piece of bamboo with holes carved out at several joints was hung on the wall of every kitchen. It was used for holding extra large chopsticks used for cooking and other utensils.

The chopstick box, *hashibako*, is an individual container for a set of chopsticks, *ohashi*. These oblong boxes are similar in appearance to a pencil box. They are usually made of bamboo or lacquered wood or papier-maché and originated in China.

Early in the nineteenth century, as the general populace enjoyed their new-found prosperity and were indulging themselves in numerous luxuries, the mundane chopstick holder began to be produced in porcelain. The most common shape is tall and rectangular or cylindrical, and the containers seen most frequently are a pierced flower design in blue and white.

Perhaps these decorative holders were first used for special occasions such as the New Year's celebration, but they soon became a common container in many households.

New Year's in Japan has a special significance, and there are many customs related to this event. Many of them pertain to food. Since there is much feasting but no cooking done for several days, the delicacies are prepared in advance and stored in stacked containers.

One of the traditional dishes is a tea made of green leaves or seaweed with a salt-pickled plum in each cup. This is called *fuku-cha*. *Fuku* means good fortune and happiness and is a character often used as a signature on the bottom of Japanese porcelain; *cha* is tea.

Otoso and *ozoni* are a must for greeting the New Year. *Otoso* is a form of saké containing special herbs and spices. *Ozoni* is a soup that includes toasted squares of *mochi*, chewy rice cakes made from steamed and pounded glutinous rice. They are the center of New Year's meals.

Each dish served during this festive season has a special meaning, such as good health, luck, good fortune, and long life. The *hashitate* will be found on every table, adding its services to the banquet.

Chopstick holders are both decorative and functional. They are attractive candleholders and can make interesting accessories on a desk or in an artist's studio for holding pencils or brushes.

Chopstick boxes are ideal pencil or stamp containers.

Chopstick holder. Blue-and-white porcelain with openwork chrysanthemum design. Late nineteenth century. H. 4 in.

HOT WATER PITCHERS—YUTO

THE JAPANESE YUTO is a hot water pitcher used in both homes and commercial establishments for many centuries. *Yu* means hot water, and *to*, a container. This water pitcher was an all-purpose object in every household and made of lacquered wood. The simple ones are finished in black or red lacquer or a combination of both. The more elaborate examples often bear a family crest in gold or have a gold lacquer finish.

In the home, one of its uses was for pouring water into a basin, the *tarai*. This was utilized for personal grooming such as washing the hands, teeth cleaning and blackening, and shaving the top of the head as well as the face. Many times the water pitcher and basin were made as a set for this use with matching decorative designs.

In the kitchen the *yuto* carried hot water from a kettle over the open-pit fire to a basin for dishwashing. In serving, it also filled multiple purposes: hot water was used for making tea; it was added to the sauce in which certain foods were prepared to make an instant, end of the meal soup; and alone it was served as an after-dinner digestive aid.

The hot water pitcher is still used commercially in many noodle shops, although some use much less beautiful aluminum kettles. Noodles are boiled, transferred to a bowl, and served with a special sauce. Once the noodles are eaten, the original, milky-colored water in which they are boiled is served in a *yuto* to be added to the sauce to make a soup.

Since buckwheat noodles were believed to have restorative powers, it became the custom when one had a cold, to have a bowl of noodles while leisurely soaking in steaming hot water at the local bathhouse. The practice was so agreeable that even without colds people enjoyed this pastime, and it remained popular until the turn of this century.

Yuto are in use in some Japanese households even today. Old ones can readily be found for sale in both antique and folk art shops. They make unique pitchers for serving hot drinks and are decorative and useful for flower and plant watering pots as well.

Hot water pitcher. Red lacquer on wood. Late eighteenth century. H. 6.2 in.

HANDLED BASINS—TSUNO-DARAI

IT IS PROBABLE that a form of the lacquered horn-handled bowl—*tsuno-darai*—developed in the Heian period (794–1185). It was used as a wash or toilet basin and was often accompanied by a matching lacquer pitcher for carrying the water.

As early as 701 A.D. lacquer art, originally imported from China, had developed sufficiently so that a government office to control the Lacquerers' Guild was formed.

As with the other arts, Buddhism fostered the development of lacquer ware, and for several centuries most of the art lacquers were made as ritual objects or accessories for this growing religion.

During the Heian period, however, the ostentatious and ceremonial ways of the court gave a major impetus to the art, and lacquer articles for personal use began to be produced.

The Heian court ladies (and men) used teeth black, the application of which could be messy as well as odoriferous, and a lacquer vessel of this type was most useful. Its name was derived from the *tsuno*, or "horns," protruding as handles, considered a symbol of the jealousy of the female sex from ancient times.

The women believers of one sect of Buddhism wore silk caps when they visited temples to stop their "horns of jealousy" from growing. From this practice came the custom of the Japanese bride wearing a similar cap on her wedding day. A form of this head covering is worn even today during the marriage ceremony.

Could it be that perhaps this type of vessel was first introduced as a daily moral reminder to the lovely ladies of the imperial court to keep their jealousy contained? Or might it first have been used for washing the hair and thus symbolically sweeping away any symptoms of this undesirable shortcoming?

Basin. Black lacquer on wood with horn-shaped handles and decorative gold *maki-e* crest. Late eighteenth century. H. 7.5 in., D. 12 in.

LACQUER WARE—NURIMONO

THE RECORDED HISTORY of lacquer in China is earlier then that of bronze. Valued at first as a protective coating, the possibilities of lacquer were very quickly exploited to decorate as well as preserve, and even materials other than wood were coated with this precious substance.

Lacquer ware, then as now, was expensive and highly prized. In this earliest period it was used for writing records of important events on bamboo slips, since the making of paper was not discovered until about 105 A.D. It was also utilized for painting carts to enhance their strength and elegance and for coating and decorating ritual vessels and burial objects as well as utensils for daily use.

From the beginning of the Warring States period (ca. 480 B.C.), lacquer ware design grew more varied and luxurious due to the demand of the rulers and aristocracy.

In Japan, the use of the sap of the *urushi* (lacquer) tree was probably a technique imported from China at an early date. During the Nara period (645–794) lacquer attained great sophistication; various pigments were added to decorate a wide variety of objects. From that time on, the Japanese developed new methods and techniques that brought lacquer to the highest degree in craftsmanship. In technical excellence it quickly surpassed its early Chinese origins.

From the rich heritage of the Japanese Edo period (1614–1868), when lacquer production was prolific, one can still find purchasable objects.

Stacked food boxes (*jubako*), make marvelous accessory trays for such personal items as scarves, jewelry, cosmetics, stationery, or cigarettes. Soup and rice bowls are ideal for snack foods, and serving trays come in assorted sizes, some large enough to convert into handsome tables. The design motifs are more often from nature: cresting waves, birds, waterfowl, butterflies, flowers, pine, and animals. Others feature geometric patterns.

Lacquer art objects, often resplendent with gold, silver, and mother-of-pearl, were once the exclusive property of the rich. One may also find exquisite pieces of folk lacquer that show the honesty and beauty of their rustic origins. Today, both the simple and the refined are a joy to own and come alive with daily use and care.

Covered bowl. *Negoro* (coral red over black) lacquer on wood. Sixteenth century. H. 3.5 in., D. 5 in.

Lidded container for cooked rice. Red lacquer on wood. Nineteenth century. H. 5 in., D. 9.6 in.

NOODLE CUPS—SOBA-CHOKO

PORCELAIN NOODLE CUPS, *soba-choko*, are charming, handleless cups, used in serving one of Japan's most popular foods.

Soba, or buckwheat noodles, is a food distinctly Japanese, enjoyed by all classes of people as both common fare and one for special occasions.

Buckwheat grew wild in Japan in olden days, but according to historical journals its cultivation was encouraged by imperial edict in 722 (during the Nara period). This was due to a serious drought that had affected the country and the fact that buckwheat can grow on both barren and fertile land.

Originally a dough was made from the buckwheat flour and small pieces boiled, which were eaten with a sauce made of soy sauce and sweet saké. It was around the seventeenth century that *kiri-soba*, or noodles cut in long strips, first appeared.

In Tokyo it is an old custom to make a gift of noodles to new neighbors when changing households. As a token of friendship, soba is presented to "three across the street and one on each side."

Throughout the world, people of different nationalities always eat something special on New Year's to assure a prosperous year to come. In Japan, on New Year's Eve, the Japanese eat "*toshikoshi-soba*," or "year-crossing noodles." According to one story, the sticky soba dough was once used by goldsmiths and silversmiths to collect scraps of gold and silver. Thus, its association with accumulating money made its eating a propitious event of the New Year.

Today, soba is served in a variety of ways, but the two most familiar are *kake-soba* and *mori-soba*. In *kake-soba* the noodles are served in a bowl of soup, while in *mori-soba* the noodles are piled up on a type of bamboo tray with sauce in a cup on the side. The noodles are picked up with chopsticks, dipped into sauce in the noodle-cup, or *soba-choko*, and eaten.

These lovely porcelain soba cups are unique, plentiful, and practical, and there are many old ones still available today. They come in varied sizes, in both blue-and-white and colored designs, and may be coupled with modern wooden or lacquer saucers for convenience of serving. Versatile soba cups are an ideal size for martinis or any drink served "on the rocks." They can also be used for soups, Japanese tea, as a dish for a fish or fruit cocktail, for desserts, or as a container for after-dinner mints or cigarettes.

Sets of soba cups (five to a set) are not always easy to find, but it is fun to build your own varied collection. Choose a color, a particular design, or a size as a theme and collect them at random.

Noodle cups. Porcelain, blue-and-white and overglaze enamels. Late nineteenth, early twentieth centuries. Average H. 3 in., D. 3.5 in.

SAKÉ BOTTLES

THE CUSTOM OF DRINKING RICE WINE, *saké*, is as old as the history of Far Eastern civilization. In the books of the ancient Chinese classics there are many references to its festive and ceremonial use. Predating written records are the gigantic bronze vessels that attest to the rice wine rituals of over three thousand years ago.

In Japan, saké was used as an offering to *kami*, "the gods," on special occasions and afterwards was shared among the people. The women controlled the home-brewed supply with a tight fist between festivals. But on these occasions it was their duty to serve and to entertain the drinking guests with songs and dances. It was expected that all would join in the revelry and become merry and drunk. Even today there is a benevolent attitude among the Japanese toward drinking and happy inebriation.

Originally brewed in the home, saké later came to be produced commercially, and itinerant saké brewers were employed by well-to-do families to make saké on their premises. It was brewed in large barrels and sent to local saké merchants or sold in bulk directly to the feudal lords for their retinue.

The shops of the saké merchants had little etiquette attached to consumption of this warming liquid, and the square wooden cup still seen today in old-fashioned saké shops and some Japanese restaurants was actually a measuring cup for the saké. It came to be used to serve the steady drinker who could only afford one cup at a time.

Even after saké was sold in glass bottles, many alert housewives, who also used saké for cooking, followed the old custom of taking their empty bottle from home. The clever ladies could then be sure of receiving an additional measure for "service."

Tokkuri are the smaller bottles in which the saké is warmed and served. These are an ideal size for individual wine carafes or bud vases.

The larger bottles, found in both pottery and porcelain, are handsome decorative objects, handy for dry flower arrangements or suitable for lamp bases.

Saké bottle or jug. Porcelain with trade name in dark blue characters. Wrapped bamboo handle. Early twentieth century. H. 14 in.

SERVING TRAYS—BON, ZEN, SANBO

SERVING TRAYS, *bon* or *zen*, are either flat, on tiny legs, or on elevated stands. Some of the more elaborate ones are done beautifully in black with gold lacquer and were handed down from old daimyo families, the regional lords of feudal Japan. Occasionally sets of trays can be found that were used to serve large groups of guests in mansions, temples, and inns. These are often finished in gleaming black or red lacquer or a combination of the two colors.

The flat trays are used for carrying food and drinks, and the others become individual table-trays at meals. In a traditional Japanese meal the food is brought in prearranged in an artistic manner on the individual, elevated trays; then the soup and rice (the only part of the meal served hot) are carried in separately.

Sanbo are small platforms or stands used to serve saké or snacks in the homes of the nobility, in restaurants, and in geisha houses. Today these stands are mostly in use in temples and shrines, where gifts of food are traditionally offered to the deities.

Though Japanese lacquer production and techniques owe a great deal to China, the Japanese quickly developed this art into one uniquely their own. Japanese lacquer in many instances became superior in quality to that of the Chinese, and lacquer became to Japan what porcelain is to China.

The golden age of lacquer in Japan could be said to be from the Momoyama through the Edo periods (1573–1868). It was during the latter period that many objects of daily use came to be extravagantly decorated in lacquer for the use of both the nobility and the newly rising merchant class.

Lacquer has a close affinity to moisture and darkness. In the present century the tombs of Ch'ang-sha in China (circa 500 B.C.) have yielded a quantity of ancient lacquer pieces in excellent condition. This is attributed to the tombs being below water level, where the objects were preserved in a state of complete saturation for more than two thousand years.

Antique lacquer trays come in a wide variety of shapes and sizes and their uses are limitless. The flat shapes are elegant serving accessories and make beautiful individual place settings on a dinner table.

They are also ideal for serving from a buffet. The smaller sizes on raised stands are lovely fruit containers, handy for holding canapés or after-dinner sweets, and are stunning serving dishes for buffet luncheons or dinners. Whatever their use, lacquer trays always enhance any setting and more often than not are reasonably priced.

Tray. Black lacquer on wood with family crest in gold *maki-e*. Early nineteenth century. 12 in. sq.

SEWING BOXES—HARIBAKO

SEWING HAS BEEN one of the Japanese lady's main pursuits since the beginning of the country's recorded history.

The Japanese sewing box is called a *haribako*. *Hari* means pin or needle, and *bako*, box. It is usually a small, square box about one foot tall, with varisized drawers to hold sewing accessories. On one side is a support that extends above the main box and holds a smaller container called a *kukedai*. *Kuke* translates, blind stitch, and a *dai* is a stand. This name originated in the practice of Japanese ladies sewing several strands of thread loosely through the pincushion in the top drawer of the *kukedai* and then looping the threads over a pin piercing the corner of the garment on which they were sewing. In this manner, the fabric could be stretched taut to facilitate doing hems and other finishing work requiring a blind stitch.

Since the sewing box was one of their few personal objects, it was often used by women of all classes to hold secret savings, which came to be called *haribako-gin*, "sewing box gold."

In this respect, the country women were much more liberated than their city sisters. Rural wives were permitted to own land and money in their own name, and they could work to increase their nest egg.

City wives had to gather their small savings from daily household expenses, which made them shrewd shoppers, a reputation they still enjoy today.

The art of sewing was so respected that there was even a special memorial service for broken needles. This was born from the ancient custom of praying for certain fish, animals, and inanimate objects that had sacrificed themselves for the well-being of humans.

In this ceremony, called *hari-kuyo*, broken needles were saved until the eighth of February every year, when they were taken to the shrine or temple to be implanted into a piece of *tofu* (bean curd) at the altar. *Tofu* was chosen for its consistency, the moral being that the needle deserved a soft berth after its hard work.

During the Edo period, this event became an important social affair, and women vied to see who could appear in the most beautiful kimono to pay homage to the instruments of their handiwork. Even now, this event is still observed in a few communities.

Old sewing boxes, in a variety of lovely natural woods, are readily available today. They are handy containers for a variety of accessories, and I know of one ingenious lady who used her *haribako* to fashion a handsome lamp base.

Sewing box. Mulberry wood with copper fittings. Late nineteenth century. H. 17.5 in.

SMOKING SETS—TABAKOBON

THE SMOKING TRAY or box—*tabakobon*—came into use in the late sixteenth century as an accessory to the Japanese pipe, called a *kiseru*.

In 1543, the Portuguese introduced two important items to Japan, the matchlock gun and tobacco. The latter enjoyed an almost immediate popularity among both women and men. By 1596, tobacco was being produced in Japan, and the Japanese pipe had been developed. This smoking pipe has a much smaller bowl than the European counterpart, and the tobacco is cut much finer to fit into it. It produces a very mild smoke of only two or three puffs. Women's pipes were smaller than those of men, and in strong contrast to the mores of their Western sisters, smoking enjoyed great popularity among all classes of ladies.

During the Edo period (1614–1868), as smoking gained in popularity, the necessary utensils were carried in on a tray, and it became a matter of etiquette to offer tobacco to visitors or friends. In the gay quarters, it was the custom for a hostess to offer a lighted pipe to visitors. This custom can be seen in its modified version even today, as the nightclub hostess or geisha attentively lights cigarettes for her guest.

With the widespread use of charcoal around the middle of the Edo period, the flat tray was exchanged for a box in which a porcelain or metal container holding charcoal on a bed of ashes was placed. Alongside was a bamboo container for tinder.

At this same time smoking boxes for the elite became increasingly more decorative, and many were done in fine lacquer or choice woods with small drawers for tobacco, a rack for the smoking pipe, and a small brazier for the charcoal. As they were basically portable, many had handles. Smoking boxes were widely used until the Meiji period, when cigarettes came into vogue. However, in a few areas *tabakobon* are still used, and you can see new ones for sale in department stores.

There are a variety of antique smoking boxes still available, and they make charming interior accessories. They may be used as portable ashtrays, can be effective as miniature planters to hold indoor greenery, and since the drawers are ideal for storing small items such as pencils, stamps, paperclips, etc., they make a picturesque and functional desk accessory.

Smoking box. Red and gold lacquer on wood; copper brazier and pipe. Late nineteenth century. H. 7 in., W. 7.5 in., D. 6.5 in.

STACKED FOOD BOXES—JUBAKO

IN JAPAN, LACQUER WARE was first used for food containers by Buddhist priests at Mt. Koya during the Kamakura period (circa 1288) but it was in the following Muromachi period (1333–1573) that the stacked food box—*jubako*—came to be made. It was convenient for serving individual meals at a banquet and later came into popular use as a tiered food storage and serving container for the New Year's season, when social and family obligations and visits allowed no time for cooking for several days. It was also used for portable meals. There were elaborately decorated sets called *hanami-ju* ("flower viewing" boxes) or *sage-ju* (carrying boxes). These were often food boxes and saké containers together in a carrying frame used for picnics, especially for cherry blossom viewing.

April is the month of cherry blossoms in Japan. The first *sakura*-viewing party was held by the Emperor Saga in 812, when the nobility and highly placed officials were invited to view the blossoms at the palace.

During the Edo period (1614–1868), when a popular culture became highly developed and leisure pursuits common, cherry blossom viewing enjoyed a great vogue. Dressed in their best finery, people of all classes went to view the beautiful flowers and eat and drink to the accompaniment of music and dance. Naturally, this pastime stimulated the production of picnic boxes, and novel and elegant containers were made.

There are many types of *jubako*. Some are square, some round, and others take unique shapes such as that of a fan. The usual are from three to five layers, although commercial establishments have those with infinite tiers and several lids. They are made of either lacquered wood or porcelain.

Old *jubako* make decorative containers for cigarettes or candy and for canapés or relishes when entertaining. With a felt, velvet, or brocade lining, they are ideal accessory trays.

Stacked food boxes. (L) Black lacquer on wood with gold *maki-e* bamboo design. Late nineteenth century. H. 9 in., W. 8.5 in. (R) White porcelain with blue flower decoration. Early twentieth century. H. 6.5 in., W. 3.5 in.

Portable food box. Black lacquer on wood with *maki-e* floral design. Pewter saké bottles. Mid nineteenth century. H. 11.5 in.

TEA BOXES—CHABAKO

THE TEA CHEST or box, *chabako*, in its modern form is of undetermined origin, but there must have been tea containers, most likely of wood and metal, from the thirteenth century on. The present tea box is a rectangular wooden box, about sixteen inches in height, lined with tin to keep moisture from reaching the tea leaves.

Although tea had been imported to Japan as early as the Nara period (645–794), it was not until 1191 that tea seeds were first brought to Japan by the Zen Buddhist priest Eisai. These first seeds were planted at the Kozan-ji temple in the western part of Kyoto. It was from there that the first tea leaves in the country were obtained.

As the tea drinking habit spread from the Zen priests to the nobility and military class, tea plants were cultivated in other areas. By the end of the Kamakura period, one hundred years later, tea drinking had become so popular that contests were held to judge the best teas, after which banquets were enjoyed by all.

Japanese green tea is a mild and fragrant drink with a very subtle flavor. According to chemical analysis, it has definite food value in that it contains both vitamins A and C. Also its iron content is believed to be an important element in purifying the blood.

Chabako are available at most any neighborhood tea store in Japan. They come in several sizes and are nominal in price. Similar to a cedar chest, they make excellent storage containers and provide good moth and mildew protection for clothing.

For children's rooms, they are ideal as toy chests. The rough exterior can easily be refinished in self-adhesive vinyl. When covered in old *obi* brocade, grass cloth, blue-and-white printed summer kimono cotton, or an interesting Japanese paper, tea boxes become conversation pieces in addition to their practicality and are ideal for use as end tables. Finishing touches may be wooden stands and glass tops made to order.

Tea box. Wood lined with tin and covered with *obi* brocade. *Obi* late nineteenth century. H. 18 in.

BOLSTERS, ARMRESTS—SOKU, KYOSOKU

SOKU AND KYOSOKU are Japanese armrests. *Soku* are like bolsters, and *kyosoku* are made of wood in rectangular or kidney shapes with legs at each end. They stand about one foot tall and sometimes there is an attached or independent pad on top. *Kyosoku* have changed little in styling through the years. The earliest examples are from the eighth century. They are in the Shosoin Imperial Treasurehouse, listed as former possessions of the Emperor Shomu. One has a phoenix design on purple silk brocade; the other is a sophisticated, multistriped brocade sewn on the bias. Similar ones are still in use today.

From the beginning, Japanese architecture has focused on a nearness to nature—gently enclosing space within a natural setting. The flooring of Japanese buildings has traditionally been *tatami*, a woven reed matting with a binding of hemp cloth. On this flooring one ate, slept, played games, meditated, and performed all the functions of daily life. One room served multiple purposes, its function changing by means of portable accessories. At night *futon*, or quilted bedding, was unrolled for sleeping. Mornings brought forth a cosmetic stand and mirror and large lacquer basins filled with water for grooming. Refreshments and meals were served on small tables, often lacquered, and armrests were familiar room furniture. They were used for both the formal seated position (knees bent, calves tucked under the haunches) and for more casual positions.

The armrest was originally a rich man's pleasure, used only by the members of the imperial court and the feudal lords. During the Edo period (1614–1868), it came into widespread use in the entertainment quarters and among the newly rich, middle-class merchants.

Most commonly seen now are the wooden armrests on legs. The finest are luxuriously lacquered, and it is not unusual to find them separated from their original silk or brocade pads.

Even today, they are unique and useful accessories for modern cushion sitting and also make interesting and handy footstools.

Armrest. Black lacquer on wood with gold *maki-e* grape and vine design. Pad covered in red *obi* brocade. Early twentieth century. H. 11.5 in.

CHESTS—TANSU

MORE THAN THREE HUNDRED YEARS ago large wooden chests of drawers and cabinets, *tansu*, were imported into Japan from Korea for use in storing clothing.

Styles were based upon class distinctions. The daimyo and the samurai class used the finest woods in cabinet styles or large four-drawer, lacquered chests often with their crests in gold on the front. Lesser ranks used chests of poorer quality, unfinished woods. Kimonos were stored in either cabinet or box style chests that were lined in *kiri* (paulownia) wood to keep moisture out. In the castles and palatial residences of the lords, the chests were never on display but stored in special *tansu* rooms. Garments were delivered as required on large trays by the servants of the household.

Prior to this time, clothing was usually stored in large, lacquered wooden boxes, which were also kept either in a separate room or in the hallway that ran adjacent to the living quarters.

In the middle Edo period (1614–1868), the Japanese began to adapt *tansu* to their own particular needs, and they came into use among the newly prominent merchant class, who used them to hold their records and the accessories of business.

The *yome-iri-dansu* (bridal chest) was part of the marriage trousseau. If the family was prosperous, the bridal or marriage chest came in three sections. If the family was not so affluent, either in wealth or rank, the middle section was omitted and more drawers added to the bottom chest.

In the top chest the accessories for the kimono were stored with handbags and other larger items behind the sliding doors. The second section was cabinet style, and kimonos were carefully folded and put on sliding trays fitted inside. The bottom chest of drawers was for undergarments.

Old chests make picturesque storage units for modern living. There are many sizes, types of wood, and styles of drawers and finishes in *tansu*, depending on the region in which they were made and their original function. Most dealers are happy to relate as much as they know about the history of antique chests they have in stock, which always adds to the pleasure of owning and using them.

Chest on wheels (*kuruma-dansu*) for valuables. Wood and iron. Mid nineteenth century. H. 36.5 in

Chest, from north-central Japan. *Keyaki* wood. Late nineteenth century. H. 37 in.

CLOTHING STANDS, TOWEL RACKS—IKO, TENUGUI-KAKE

THE CLOTHING STAND, *iko*, has been a part of Japanese interior furniture for many centuries. Its predecessor came from China, where a rack of similar shape was in use as early as the Shang dynasty (1200 B.C.).

Iko are about five feet in height, with two vertical poles or planks in stands and a crossbar at the top. As the wood has to be smoothly finished in order not to snag the luxurious kimono silk, they are usually finished in gleaming black lacquer. Several partially folded kimonos can be draped over the stand to test color and pattern combinations, or a single kimono can be hung by inserting the crossbar through the sleeves. A smaller version of the clothing stand is used for accessories, and another one is a towel rack, called *tenugui-kake*.

The clothing rack probably arrived on Japanese shores along with the great influx of Chinese T'ang culture during the Nara period (645–794). Japanese costume of this era was totally inspired by the styles from the continent, and rigid court etiquette was established concerning the type of clothing to be worn for each occasion. Colors, too, were restricted to use by specific ranks within the court. It was decreed that below the rank of prince the nobles should wear—according to rank—purple, lavender, crimson, Indian red, cherry, mulberry, dark blue, light blue, leaf green, and grass green. The paler the color the lower the rank.

By the following Heian period (794–1185), when the twelve-layer kimono became fashionable—and it was not unusual for court ladies to wear as many as twenty layers at one time—the clothing stand was certainly in widespread use within imperial court circles. Great care was given to the selection of harmonious colors, and each color and flower pattern had its appropriate occasion and season. It is certain that a great deal of draping and discussing were carried on daily. From the famous Lady Murasaki's dairy we learn about one unfortunate lady, who, in her appearance before the emperor made an error in dress, heaven forbid! It was a small one—at the wrist it seems one color was "a little too pale." Ah, the mortification!

In the Momoyama period (1573–1614), painted screens that depict kimonos displayed on racks were made. They are called "Whose Sleeves," and show popular kimono patterns of the day.

In the Genroku era (1688–1703), it was fashionable to gaily display a lady's wardrobe by hanging her kimonos over ropes around a picnic pavilion at cherry-viewing time.

Such clothing and towel stands are still in use in Japan today. The smaller sizes are convenient for accessories such as necklaces and scarves. They also make graceful, unique towel racks for a dressing room.

Accessory stand. Black lacquer on wood with gold *maki-e* decoration; etched metal fittings. Early nineteenth century. H. 24.5 in.

HEARTH HANGERS—JIZAI-KAGI

THE ADJUSTABLE HEARTH HANGER, *jizai-kagi*, made of combinations of wood, metal, and bamboo, has been a familiar sight in Japan for many centuries.

This hanger is attached to a large overhead beam and extends down from the ceiling to a few feet above the hearth. It is sometimes made of wood, or many times is an iron rod or chain. Often the wooden or metal extensions are sheathed in a long bamboo rod. Near the bottom is a large, horizontal balance made of wood carved into various shapes—the most common being giant wooden hooks, fish, and fans. Below this is a large metal hook used for suspending the kettle or pot over the hearth.

A few of these are still in use in country homes today. Their origin is obscure, but it is likely that they were brought into the country in prehistoric days, since almost every ancient culture has a facsimile.

The open hearth, *irori*, was the first heating system in ancient Japan and used by all classes of people. It is constructed by making a square hole in the center of a room, lining it with wood or stone and filling it with ash, on which wood or charcoal is burned. This hearth is also used for auxiliary cooking, and a large kettle with hot water for tea or an iron pot containing soups or stews is suspended over the fire from the hearth hanger. This adjustable hanger can be raised or lowered, according to the amount of heat desired.

The open hearth room is the center of family living in the country-side, and on cold nights families often place sweet potatoes on the hot ashes to bake or warm their rice cakes over the fire. Around the hearth meals are taken, visitors entertained, and many times at night bedding is spread for cosy winter sleeping.

The picturesque Japanese thatched roof, still seen in the country-side, goes hand in hand with the open hearth. It is laid very thick and keeps the house warm in winter and cool in summer. The smoke from the hearth keeps the reeds dry and also drives out insects. This keeps the roof in good condition and gives it a longer life. Many of these roofs are over a hundred years old, but they are no longer permitted in cities, since they are too easily inflammable.

Hearth hangers may be found in many curio shops today, since the old open hearth is rapidly being replaced in Japan by modern heating. They can be hung over old *hibachi*, or used over a rock garden or in a corner to hang containers of flowers or plants. A large one makes a beautiful decorative accessory in a stairwell. The old bronze and iron kettles that hang on *jizai-kagi* also make interesting room accessories.

Two wooden hearth hanger (*jizai-kagi*) fixtures. The fish symbolizes good fortune. Late nineteenth century.

HIBACHIS: PORCELAIN, WOOD

HIBACHIS ARE TRADITIONAL JAPANESE CHARCOAL BRAZIERS. They are still used as heating units in the countryside of Japan today, though their use is diminishing. There are two different types of hibachi: large porcelain or pottery pots, and wooden boxes with metal liners, often very refined in workmanship, with special little drawers for tobacco, eyeglasses, paper, and other oddments used mainly by the head of the household.

The hibachi's ancestor dates from the Heian period (794–1185). Called either *hioke* or *hibitsu* (derived from the words *hi*, "fire," *oki*, "tub," and *bitsu*, "chest"), they were metal buckets set in cypress wood and fitted with a pottery liner to hold wood for burning. In those early times, only the elite could afford such a brazier. However, in the seventeenth century, when charcoal became readily available, wooden hibachis with copper liners became common household items.

Of all the many styles, the Edo period *naga-hibachi*, a rectangular wooden box, is the most common. These were used primarily in homes, which often doubled as shops and businesses. The place before the drawers was reserved for the father, since from this position he could receive guests or customers and have his necessary sundries at hand. Smaller, more portable hibachis were used in other rooms.

There are two main shapes of *naga-hibachi*. The *daiwa-hibachi* with a thick shelf surrounding the fire box was used in the Kyoto-Osaka area. The *Edo-hibachi* with sides extending straight down was used in Edo (Tokyo) and vicinity.

During the Meiji Restoration, Japanese export business flourished, and along with it, the porcelain business boomed. Porcelain ware flooded the domestic market as well, and during that time porcelain hibachis, *binkake*, became the thing to have in every home. Most of the blue-and-white patterns that decorated the hibachis were hand-painted by the famous craftsmen of Kyushu, but stencil techniques were also employed to speed up production and so meet consumer demand.

Today hibachis are popular among nearly everyone interested in Japanese antiques. No wonder, because the wooden ones make handsome side tables, and the porcelain hibachis serve perfectly as planters—for perhaps one of your bamboo plants.

Hibachi. Tokyo area style, *keyaki* wood with copper liner and fittings. Late nineteenth century. H. 15 in.

Hibachi. Kyoto style, *keyaki* wood trimmed in black persimmon. Late nineteenth century. H. 14 in.

LACQUERED (DAIMYO) HIBACHIS

The Heian period (794–1185) was one of great opulence, and it is probable that the lacquered hibachi was first made at that time. The earliest hibachi shape was a round metal pan, surrounded by wood, with a pottery liner in which to burn the firewood.

In 1142 A.D. the Emperor Konoe ordered the entire furniture of the palace to be done in a speckled gold lacquer, called *nashiji*. However, lacquer production remained confined to the exclusive use of the imperial court, a few great feudal lords, and the wealthy Buddhist temples for several centuries.

During the Muromachi period (1333–1573), the Ashikaga shoguns were great patrons of the arts, and Japanese artists began to achieve a higher social status and be known by name. It was also a time when lacquer art schools and families began to develop, and a high point in lacquer design was reached.

In the following Momoyama period (1573–1614) the arts were patronized by the military rulers as well as the local feudal lords, daimyo, who lived in luxury in large castles and surrounded themselves with fine arts and artists. It was from these daimyo that the lacquer hibachi received its name. During this period a wide range of utilitarian articles developed, including furniture suitable for lacquer decoration.

A further acceleration came in the Edo period (1614–1868), when the lords were required to spend half the year in Edo and maintain splendid mansions there in addition to their home castles. Lacquer production flourished, and artists, who usually had no status, were frequently given the rank of a samurai or titles equal to those of the high Buddhist clergy.

The daimyo hibachi is usually square in shape with four gracefully curved legs. It is lacquered in black or occasionally brown, and intricate geometrical or floral patterns were painted on the ground in gold lacquer. Sizes vary from around twelve up to twenty inches square. This made them easily transportable for use in the numerous chambers of the castles and mansions.

Lacquered braziers are still to be found, though rare, and can be put to modern use in several ways. They make handsome serving trays on a buffet table and charming planters or flower containers.

Daimyo hibachi. Black lacquer on wood with gold *maki-e* decoration, copper fittings. Early nineteenth century. 7.5 × 15 × 15 in.

MINIATURE HIBACHIS, HANDWARMERS— TE-ABURI HIBACHI

THE TE-ABURI HIBACHI is a small portable fireplace that was originally transported from room to room and around which the family and guests could warm their hands and drink tea. It was made in many materials—bronze, iron, porcelain, earthenware, or wood lined in copper. According to the purpose, a variety of sizes was used.

In Japan, prior to modern times, many ways were devised to give warmth during the cold winter, although no attempt was made to heat rooms. The construction of the houses in wood, clay, and paper offered little protection from the elements. Also, living with nature was considered an integral part of daily life, and it was not unusual for all the doors to be thrown open to enjoy a beautiful snowfall on a winter's day or the rising moon on a cold, clear night.

Various personal heating units were used for warmth, most of them utilizing charcoal.

Custom demanded that whenever a visitor arrived, the first act of hospitality would be to set a hibachi in front of him. This was also true of commercial shops. Customers would either be invited to sit around a hibachi that was present or one would be brought and placed before them. This was as much a part of the greeting as was the serving of tea, still observed today. Some families could boast that their hibachi fires had been burning for hundreds of years, indicating that they were always prepared to receive guests in proper fashion.

The *irori* is the open-pit hearth around which the family cooked, slept, and warmed themselves.

The *kotatsu* is a wooden rack placed over the *ro* (a small hearth) and covered with a quilt. The family then sits around the hearth with their legs and feet under the quilt for warmth. Electric *kotatsu* are still very popular today.

For bitter cold nights, there was an *anka*, or foot warmer. This was an earthenware pot containing charcoal ashes covered by a wooden box and coverlet. In modern times a *yutanpo*, or hot water bottle, made of porcelain or metal came to be used.

The *kairo* was a small metal container in which powdered charcoal was placed, and it was used as a bosom, pocket, or tummy warmer.

Modern heating has replaced the hibachi in most Japanese homes, so these attractive, utilitarian objects can be found in antique and second-hand furniture shops.

The larger hibachis are easily converted to coffee and side tables, while the smaller types are ideal flower containers, planters, or fruit bowls.

Miniature hibachis fitted as smoking boxes. (L) *Keyaki* wood trimmed in persimmon. Late nineteenth century. H. 8 in. (R) Wooden box with porcelain bowl for ashes and charcoal; bamboo cylinder for refuse. Early twentieth century. H. 3.5 in.

LAMPS, LANTERNS—ANDON

THE JAPANESE INDOOR LANTERN is called an *andon*. It consists of a wooden frame covered with paper and open above and below. Inside is a tiny saucer holding vegetable oil, and a wick is placed a ring of iron or on a shelf built into one corner of the saucer.

The vegetable oil lamp was the earliest source of meagre nighttime illumination in ancient Japan. The first model was a simple wooden tripod with a shallow pottery dish perched on top to hold the oil and wick.

In the Heian period (794–1185), a paper cone was attached to a wooden stick on a stand to form a shade for the light. However, these were in use only among the nobility. During the Muromachi period (1333–1573), a lady's lamp was used, which featured a large round wooden disc attached to one side of the rod and stand. This reflected the light in one direction only. Many times the wood was painted with delicate flowers, the chrysanthemum being a favorite.

Many types of wood, paper, lacquer, and iron lampstands developed, the materials and construction determined by their intended use. Some were for religious ceremonies, some for the inner rooms and hallways of the nobility and aristocracy, and a few for outdoor use. Others were designed exclusively for the use of either men or women.

The Japanese paper lantern, *chochin*, used outdoors, derived its name from the Chinese term for a hanging lantern. Lanterns are closely associated with the popular Japanese Bon Festival celebrated in midsummer. The term *obon* is a slang expression of the original Sanskrit term meaning a service held by the relatives of the dead who wished to express their gratitude to the departed. It was commonly believed that on this day the spirits of the dead return to their earthly homes, and therefore a feast was prepared and lanterns were hung to light the way. As time went on, it also became a celebration of homecoming for the living.

Lantern floating was a beautiful ending to the festival and can still be seen occasionally. Hundreds of little floats are lighted with candles and glide down rivers or to the sea to guide the spirits back to earth. The sight of this multitude of bobbing lights is breathtaking.

The current shape of the Japanese *andon*, a framework of painted or lacquered wood with pasted paper panels, came into use in the Edo period (1614–1868), when lamps and vegetable-wax candles were first used by the common people. Sometimes old books or posters have been used for the paper covering, adding a picturesque flavor to the lamps.

These old night lights make attractive lamps when wired for modern lighting. Most styles are refreshingly naive, with bold, classic, and simple lines. Many have tiny drawers in the base, formerly for the wicks, and they are usually finished in black, red, or brown lacquer.

Lantern. Red lacquer on wood. Late nineteenth century. H. 13 in.

Oil lamp with mouse decoration. Metal and wood. Late nineteenth century. H. 16.5 in.

GAGAKU AND NOH MASKS

NOH IS A POETIC DANCE drama that came into its traditional form in the late fourteenth century. The stage, dance, and chanted poetry are stylized to the point of being pure abstraction. The *shite*, or main actor, glides across the stage as if cloud borne, the only sounds being the rustle of his elaborate costume coupled with the austere notes of the accompanying chant and instruments.

The earliest form of music and dance recorded in Japan is called *kagura*. These religious dances were performed by Shinto priests and priestesses to call forth the gods.

During the fourth and fifth centuries, as most of Japan became united under the Yamato imperial rulers in Nara, regional folk dances were performed annually at court when tributary offerings were made. These became part of the colorful court ritual and thus were preserved.

From the seventh century through the early part of the Heian period (794–1185), foreign dances and music were imported from India, China, and Korea and incorporated with the native Japanese songs and dances to produce the court mustic called *gagaku*. The most important forms of dance and music that were introduced at this time were *gigaku*, a masked Buddhist ritual (now extinct), *bugaku*, employing masked court dancers, and *sangaku*, a type of mime and acrobatic entertainment for commoners that later became the basis for the Noh drama.

Little is known about the *gigaku* ritual, but more than 150 masks used in this ceremony are preserved in the Shosoin Imperial Treasurehouse in Nara. These include such types as lion heads, bird-beaked heads, demons, and many superhuman beings.

The dances of *bugaku* fall into four general categories: literary dances, running dances, warrior dances, and child dances. *Bugaku* masks, too, are often exaggerated, with large noses, some in bright red, and many depicting various Asian peoples of historic times.

The Noh dance drama became strictly formalized in the Edo period (1614–1868). In Noh, the mask is all important, and there are about fifty different kinds in use today. They are first sculpted from wood and then covered with multiple coats of gesso and lacquer. Making a

Noh mask is an exacting skill, and there are only a few craftsmen today who are considered qualified in this art. The actors say, "a Noh play begins with the mask," and the individuality of the actor is given up when he puts it on. Even the interpretation of the part he plays must be governed by the subtleties of the mask he has chosen.

In the early period of development, Noh masks were closer to those of *gigaku* and *bugaku* and therefore very exotic. But as Noh developed, it quickly became an aristocratic entertainment and began to take on elegance and an atmosphere of Zen Buddhism. Therefore the masks became more and more refined and expressed a mystic and quiet beauty.

Antique Noh masks are almost unobtainable today, since they are passed down from one generation to another among Noh actors and highly prized. Replicas and copies of famous masks are available in a few antique shops.

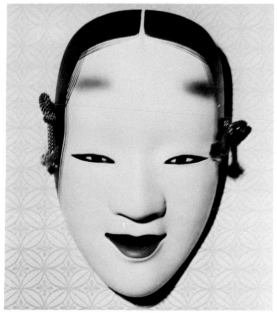

Noh mask of young woman (*waka-onna*). Colored lacquer on wood.

MUSICAL INSTRUMENTS

THE MELODIOUS RUNS of a flute, the resonant pounding of drums, and the twang of stringed instruments are familiar sounds of Japanese music heard throughout the countryside during festival times.

The six-holed bamboo flute called *Yamato-bue* is one of the few musical instruments believed to have originated in Japan. The other is the six-string cithern called the *wagon*. Representations of these and percussion instruments have been found on *haniwa* figures from the Tumulus period (ca. 200–552), and they are used in the earliest known Japanese musical form, called *kagura*, or "god music." This music is played for the sacred dances of the same name at Shinto ceremonies and festivals.

Most other Japanese musical instruments owe their origins to other cultures. The Japanese biwa came originally from India and China, and playing it was an important social grace in the courts of the late Nara and Heian periods.

A different type of *biwa* playing developed in southern Kyushu, where blind priests began playing *biwa* to accompany their singing of sutras. These singing priests led a wandering life and were accorded a great deal more freedom than the general populace. Therefore, they were often utilized as spies during the unrest of the Kamakura period (1185–1333).

The same thing was true of another group, the *komuso* of the much later Edo era (1614–1868). These were mostly masterless samurai-turned-priests, who wore basketlike hats for traveling incognito and played the *shakuhachi*, a strong, bamboo flute that could also double as a weapon.

The word *koto* was used originally as a generic term for all stringed instruments, but its modern connotation is a thirteen-stringed instrument using bridges of ivory, wood, or plastic.

The *koto*, like the *biwa*, was considered an important part of court life during the Heian period, and there is much literature alluding to beautiful ladies and the glorious tones they could coax from this Japanese harp. In Edo times, it gained fresh popularity among the lonely wives and consorts of lords left as hostages in the capitol while their masters returned to the provincial estates.

The *shamisen* claims the latest arrival in Japan in 1592. Its predecessor, the *jabisen* of the Ryukyu Islands, is a three-stringed instrument with a small wooden bridge, covered in snakeskin and played with a pick much like a banjo. After a few *biwa* artists started experimenting with it, numerous modifications were made, and it became one of the most popular and versatile instruments in the world of Japanese music.

Learning to play one of these Asian instruments brings its own rewards. Older ones have an intrinsic value for workmanship alone and often are inlaid with shell and lacquer. Most conjure forth exotic visions and sounds of an age long passed.

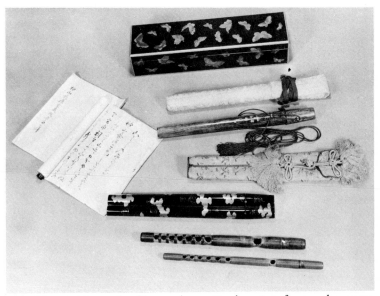

Pair of flutes with wood and lacquer boxes. Bamboo. Late fourteenth century. L. approx. 15 in.

FOLK PAINTING—OTSU-E, EMA

Two types of Japanese folk painting that developed in the early Edo period (1614–1868), are *Otsu-e* and *ema*.

Otsu is a small town on the shores of scenic Lake Biwa on the old main road to Kyoto. *Otsu-e*, or pictures from Otsu, were originally made as souvenirs for visitors traveling on this route. These pictures were naive, roughly created representations of Buddhistic deities, kabuki heroes, beautiful women, genre scenes, and folk gods. Animal motifs were popular, too, especially as additions to the main theme, the cock and hen being favorites. Often moral sayings or poems were written on the pictures. In the last phase of *Otsu-e*, they were regarded as charms, and many weird demons were depicted.

The paintings were most often done on coarse brown paper covered with a manila-colored clay called *odo*, which coated the surface like a wash. The subject was painted in brilliant mineral pigments in a spectrum of colors similar to those used in many Korean folk pictures. Bold outlines and minor details were added in a rich black. These mineral paints retain their original brightness and vivacity even after a century or more, although the paint has a tendency to flake.

Ema are votive pictures, usually of horses, painted on wood. They are often seen in Shinto shrines and Buddhist temples.

When a special favor is desired, one of these pictures is presented, along with the prayer, to a temple or shrine. It had long been a custom for live horses to be given to shrines as offerings to the gods, and white horses are presented even today. Since few could afford such a valuable object, by giving a votive picture the common people could participate more directly in the rituals of Buddhism and Shintoism.

Although the word *ema* literally means "horse picture," there are many other subjects represented. Some are of dieties, others genre scenes, and many are calligraphy. Food, flowers, and fish are popular also, since they are considered proper offerings to the gods.

Ema are usually crude portrayals, but many pulsate with a freshness, and animation that reveals the naive talent in common men.

Both *Otsu-e* and *ema* are interesting and colorful folk art still available (especially in the countryside) and priced considerably lower than Japanese fine art when they can be found.

Ōtsu-e painting. Color on paper. The Thunder God attempting to retrieve his drum. Early nineteenth century. 25 × 9.5 in.

LITERATI PAINTING—NANGA

THE JAPANESE LITERATI PAINTING SCHOOL called *nanga* ("southern painting") or *bunjinga* ("literati painting"), began around the mid eighteenth century. It was a Chinese inspired movement based on literati painting styles of the Sung, Yüan, and Ming dynasties.

The outside influences that contributed to the creation of this new school in Japan were an influx of immigrant painters from China (many Zen priest-painters) and the importation of painting instruction manuals such as the famous *Mustard Seed Garden*. These block-printed instruction books offered a new viewpoint for studying Chinese Sung, Yüan, and Ming painting styles.

At the same time, Japanese artists were dissatisfied with the official Kano school of painting, which had been the major style for almost three hundred years. The original, vigorous monumental style had, by this time, settled into a stilted pattern. It had become so academic that the paintings were lifeless and stereotyped.

The term "literati" is a misnomer if the Japanese painters are compared to their Chinese counterparts. The Chinese literati was just that, an amateur scholar-painter for whom painting was a cultural pursuit. Any mention of professionalism or, heaven forbid, money for his efforts was to be studiously avoided.

Japanese *nanga* painters were in quite a different position. Although most of them were cultured gentlemen well versed in the Chinese arts, they were also largely professionals who were dependent upon painting for their livelihood.

The subject matter of Japanese literati painting was principally one of landscapes and the "Four Gentlemen": orchid, bamboo, plum, and chrysanthemum.

Landscapes were often composed of stark rocks and jagged cliffs not usually seen in Japan, and Chinese figures and poetry were also often included.

In modern Japan, there are still many examples of literati art, much of it on hanging scrolls and some on screens and sliding doors. Though it has only recently been looked upon as an art form that is validly Japanese in style and execution if not inspiration, and because it is a relatively young movement, prices are still sometimes rather reasonable.

Painting by Kenkadō (1735–1802). Colors on paper. 52 × 12.25 in.

SLIDING DOORS—FUSUMA

SLIDING DOORS, *fusuma*, contain some of the finest examples of the art of Japanese painting.

In ancient times Buddhist painting formed the nucleus of Japanese art, but by the early eighth century secular subjects began to appear. Painting on walls, doors, and screens existed in Japan since the Nara period (645-794). However, aside from a few screen panels stored in the Shosoin Imperial Treasurehouse, which show a strong influence of the Chinese T'ang dynasty, the earliest extant examples of true Japanese style painting, *Yamato-e*, are from the Heian period (794-1185). Flowers of the four seasons, court scenes, and landscapes were popular topics for artists of that day.

The idea of monumental art enveloping the viewer had its Asian origins in the Indian caves of Ajanta and the Tun-huang caves in China (circa 5th, 6th centuries A.D.).

In Japan, art was always an integral part of architecture, and painting was considered of primary importance in filling the large panels and movable walls of numerous rooms in temples, shrines, castles, and mansions of nobles and powerful warriors.

Although paintings on walls and doors existed from early times, most of it has been lost.

Late in the Muromachi period (1333-1573), an artist named Kano Motonobu introduced a combination of the Zen monochromatic art with its strong ink brushstrokes (originally imported from China) with the more delicate lines, but vivid colors of the native Japanese *Yamato-e*. In the following Momoyama period (1573-1614), his grandson Kano Eitoku brought the style to full fruition. The screens and sliding doors of the Momoyama era, mostly executed on gold foil backgrounds, are considered a golden age of Japanese painting.

Today it is still possible to find bits of this monumental art form on antique sliding doors that have original paintings on silk, paper, wood, or gold or silver foil. They make stunning decorative pieces and can be used in their original mountings as panels or remounted into folding screens.

Sliding door painting. Colors on paper mounted on wood. Late nineteenth century. H. 68 in.

HANGING SCROLLS—KAKEMONO

THE EARLY HISTORY of Japanese painting is closely related to the importation of Buddhism in the sixth century. Almost all subject matter
remained religious until the Heian period (794-1185), when *Yamato-e*,
or Japanese style painting, introduced scenes from literature, seasonal
subjects from nature, and a small amount of portraiture.

The *kakemono*, or hanging scroll, came into a place of its own in
Japan during the following Kamakura era (1185-1333). With the arrival
of Zen Buddhism, the Chinese art of monochrome ink painting was
adapted to the Japanese taste. Subject matter broadened, and landscapes
in particular became frequent subjects. The *shiga-jiku* was developed,
shi meaning poetry and *jiku* meaning a hanging scroll. These paintings
with poetic inscriptions were done mainly by Zen priests.

In the following Muromachi period (1333-1573) the cult of tea came
into popularity. Its rules for environment and architecture integrated
the use of Zen art into the tea ritual. The focal point of the tea room or
house was the *tokonoma*, an alcove that contained the hanging scroll
and a flower arrangement. The scroll was carefully chosen to convey
the mood of the tea ritual performed.

After the Muromachi period, painting became centered around the
styles of individual artists and their followers, and artistic lineages
such as the Kano and Tosa schools arose. A cultural awakening
among the common people widened the range of art lovers and promoted the eatablishment of art purely for its own sake.

Kakemono are such scroll paintings on paper or silk mounted on richly
colored brocades to be hung on a wall. They are easy to change and
store in their original form or they may be framed. Subject matter
includes landscapes, Buddhist deities, birds and flowers, scenes from
stories and myths, and portraits. Taking time to browse and unroll
them can reap great rewards. They may be used as single art objects,
or similar sizes can form a wall unit.

The two small tabs that hang down in front were longer at one time
and used to tie the scroll securely. These *futai* no longer have any
practical use, but remain a part of the *kakemono* mounting design.

Painting, Nagasaki school. Colors on silk. Early nineteenth century. 37.5 × 16 in.

SCREENS—BYOBU

THE WORD BYOBU literally translated means "protection from the wind." Japanese screens were used as room dividers, to ward off drafts, as backdrops on ceremonial occasions, and, in general, as movable walls. Not only was their folding construction handy, but the screens' surface offered a perfect vehicle for painting to enhance interiors.

Folding screens were introduced to Japan from China and Korea around the seventh century. As in the case of lacquer ware, screens developed in Japan far beyond their original, continental forms. It was not long before they were being taken as gifts by the Japanese envoys to the Chinese court, where they were much appreciated.

The earliest screens were painted on separate panels, which were hinged together with leather or cloth thongs pulled through holes at the edge of each wooden frame. The oldest extant Japanese screens are in the Shosoin Imperial Treasurehouse in Nara and date from around 752 A.D. These consist of paintings on paper and silk and panels of woven fabric. While almost all early Japanese art was centered around Buddhism, the subject matter of these screens is uniquely secular and includes palace scenes, landscapes, poetry, natural themes such as animals, birds, flowers and grasses, and human figures.

A Korean technical innovation introduced in the mid fourteenth century hinged the screen panels together with paper and offered one continuous surface on which to paint. This opportunity for new formats and changes in composition eventually brought the art of Japanese screen painting to its zenith.

The introduction of firearms to Japan by the Portuguese in the mid sixteenth century revolutionized warfare and, with it, architecture, ushering in a golden age of screen painting during the Momoyama period (1573–1614). The monumental (and drafty) castles, made necessary by the use of guns, were perfect for large, lavishly decorated screens; the liberal use of gold backgrounds not only symbolized the strength and wealth of the new warlords but also, more practically, served to reflect light and illuminate the vast, gloomy interiors.

The screen painters of the Edo period (1614–1868) continued the Momoyama traditions; it is primarily the screens of this later period and the following Meiji that are still available in Japan today.

Screen, Rimpa school. Six panels; colors on gold foil. Early nineteenth century.
68 × 110 in.

Screen. *Tagasode* ("Whose Sleeves"). Six panels; colors on silver foil. Late eighteenth century. 56 × 105 in.

ZEN PAINTING—ZENGA

"ZENGA ARE PICTORIAL EXPRESSIONS of the Zen experience . . ." executed by Zen painter-priests.

Zen is one of hundreds of Buddhist sects. Yet it has had a greater impact on Japanese culture than all others combined. This influence extends to the fields of literature, calligraphy, drama, painting, architecture, and decorative arts through utensils produced especially for the tea ceremony. These were crafted in lacquer, porcelain, pottery, wood, bamboo, etc.

It was during the sixth century that the Indian patriarch Bodhidharma introduced Zen Buddhism to China. The Indian teachings were absorbed by the native Chinese philosophies of Taoism and Confucianism, and so it was eventually this three-part mixture that came to Japan as Zen.

Through the practice of Zen meditation, the initiate pursues the state of Enlightenment, to assimilate and become one with nature and so directly experience the great truth of the universe.

The subject matter of *Zenga* can be roughly divided into three categories: landscapes, Taoist and Buddhist figures, and *koan* pictures.

Landscapes depicted the Zen idea that a single landscape painting can be a pictorial embodiment of the essential Buddha-nature and thereby be a key in the search for Enlightenment. Birds, flowers, and landscapes accompanied by a *san*, or poetic inscription, were characteristic of this kind of painting.

The Taoist and Buddhist figures were used to give expression to a set of ideas that were the essence of Zen. One of the most popular figures is Hotei, characterized by his protruding belly and the sack in which he carries his earthly belongings. While at first glance he seems an unlikely candidate for the embodiment of Zen ideals, he is said to have wandered the land, free of all desires and in perfect harmony with nature, preaching as he went.

Zen *koan* pictures represent questions from a Zen master to his disciples to be pondered and answered by means of meditation. They try to depict that flash of inspiration that was the door to enlightenment. Only a master who had attained this state was in a position to portray it, and therefore these pictures are very rare.

Sanskrit character meaning universal purification from evil, by Jiun (1718–1804). Ink on paper. 34 × 11.75 in.

SCULPTURE

JAPANESE SCULPTURE is essentially religious in nature.

At the dawn of Japanese history, in the Neolithic Age, strange and exaggerated figurines, five to six inches in height, were produced for some religious purpose. Called *dogu*, these clay (and, rarely, stone) figurines, in the shape of humans and animals, are the earliest known examples of Japanese sculpture.

From the third to the fifth centuries, sculpture took the form of three-dimensional earthenware mortuary figures called *haniwa*. Some were fashioned after men and women, some animals, and others were objects such as houses, weapons, and boats. Each one was fitted with a hollow cylindrical base that could be stuck into the earth, and they were positioned in groups around grave mounds. Their exact purpose is a mystery, but it is thought they were made to console the dead.

When Buddhism was introduced to Japan, a new religious art was born. Buddhist sculptors and sculptures were sent to Japan from China and Korea to promote this new art form, and these influences, mingled with native concepts, produced a particularly Japanese expression of Buddhist sculptural art. Most of Japan's antique sculpture consists of Buddhist deities.

Many of the early Buddhist images were cast in bronze and gilded, but wood was the usual medium for Japanese sculpture. Clay and dry lacquer were also popular materials for the boldly colored, vigorous sculpture created during Japan's "golden age of sculpture" in the Nara period (645-794). These methods were subsequently dropped during the following Heian period in favor of wood. The style, influenced by Chinese T'ang dynasty art, became softer, rounder, and more intricate in detail. The next major sculptural era was the Kamakura period (1185-1333). There was a renaissance of the Nara period styles in addition to a new trend toward realism. At the end of this period, however, painting replaced sculpture as the highest form of Japanese art, and this trend continued until modern times.

The finest Japanese sculpture falls in the category of officially designated National Treasures rather than collectible antiques, the most outstanding examples belonging to the Todai-ji, Horyu-ji, and Kofu-ku-ji temples in Nara.

However, small bronze and wooden votive figures used in smaller temples long since destroyed and in home shrines are charming and still available.

For serious collectors a few examples of Heian and Kamakura sculpture can be found in top dealers' galleries.

Bodhisattva. Wood. Twelfth century. H. 16 in.

PATRON SAINTS—JIZO

IN JAPAN, Jizo is the patron saint of children, farmers, and common people and is probably one of the most popular deities in the land. Stone Jizo statues are found in temples, small huts, by the roadside, and in wooden form in homes. Monklike in appearance, Jizo is usually clothed in a simple, long robe with only the feet and hands exposed; his head is always bald.

Jizo came with Buddhism from China, where he was originally known as the guardian of children. In Japan his powers were expanded considerably. He took on many names and protective functions, depending on people's various needs.

It is believed that Jizo has the power to save people from earthquakes, fire and other calamities, to remove splinters, thorns, any foreign object, and in general to protect travelers.

The Amagoi Jizo, a rain-praying Jizo, is worshiped throughout the countryside. He is the farmers' special guardian, bringing rain in times of drought. Prayer ceremonies differ in each locality. In some places Jizo is immersed in a river; more often (and more easily since these stone figures are heavy) water is poured over the head. Elsewhere mud is splashed on the face so the Jizo will summon rain to wash it off. Also popular among farmers is the rice-planting Jizo.

Occasionally a Jizo will be seen tied with layers of rope. When valuables are stolen, one customarily reports the loss to the Jizo and binds him with ropes promising to free him when the thief is caught. Not all thieves are apprehended, so the statue usually remains bound in many layers of rope, and thus he is called Shibarare Jizo, or Bound Jizo.

Sometimes parents place pebbles on the head, shoulders, and base of the Jizo. Each little stone represents a prayer for the salvation of children who have been taken away by death.

If you wish to ask Jizo a favor or thank him for one granted, you may follow the Japanese custom by dressing him with aprons or other articles of clothing.

Jizo. Carved stone. Nineteenth century. H. 20 in.

WOODBLOCK PRINTS—UKIYO-E, HANGA

THE WORD *ukiyo-e* is associated with colorful woodblock prints representative of the "floating world" of old Edo during the seventeenth, eighteenth, and early nineteenth centuries. In its earliest connotation the term was linked with Buddhism and meant the transitory nature of existence. In the seventeenth century, when it came to be connected with the art of the day, it also took on added meanings such as being "up-to-date," "stylish," and even "risqué."

Arts closely associated in their developing stages with *ukiyo-e* woodblock prints were the printing of books and the kabuki theater. Though books had been printed before 1600, it was only during the seventeenth century, with the advent of the Edo period, that a literate class of any size was formed, and these people, eager to be educated, uplifted, or merely amused, formed the first real public for printed books. Some of the earliest *ukiyo-e* prints were produced as illustrations for these books.

In early kabuki theater of the time, the actors became popular figures of the day and were one of the most frequent subjects of early *ukiyo-e*.

Torii Kiyonobu is generally credited with popularizing *shibai-e*, "theater prints," and founding the Torii line of artists (still active today), all dedicated to producing theater and actor prints and posters. Shunsho broke away from this school and founded a new school of actor print design that focused on realistic facial features. Sharaku appeared upon the scene for a brief period of ten months to turn out about 140 actor prints, some of which are considered masterpieces. His identity and personal life are still unknown. The most popular portraitist of kabuki actors in the late eighteenth and early nineteenth centuries was Toyokuni I. Many undated theater prints have been pinpointed in time by checking in the old theatrical records on the actors and the parts they played.

The other most popular theme of early *ukiyo-e* was called *bijinga*, or pictures of beautiful women, mostly highly placed courtesans. Of the early period, Harunobu excelled in giving great sensitivity to his beauties, and later Kiyonaga, Utamaro, and Eisen were incomparable in their own renditions of exotically beautiful effects and treatment of feminine allure.

Landscapes came into a new prominence in the early 1800s through the masterly art of Hokusai and Hiroshige, both of whom also produced notable bird-and-flower and genre prints.

Shunga (erotic prints), *Nagasaki-e* and *Yokohama-e* (prints depicting foreigners), and *sumo-e* (prints of sumo wrestlers), along with narrative and historic prints, are other categories of *ukiyo-e*, the people's art of the Edo period.

Woodblock print, by Hiroshige (1797–1858). Japanese poet Narihira passing Mt. Fuji on his travels. 27 × 9.5 in.

ACTOR PRINTS—SHIBAI-E

SHIBAI-E, PRINTS DEPICTING ACTORS or scenes from the kabuki theater, were one of the earliest types of *ukiyo-e* prints produced.

The kabuki theater was the rage of the day, along with the gay quarters of Yoshiwara. Fans not only collected prints of their favorite actors in roles for which they were famous, but it became fashionable among both men and women to emulate the players in actions, dress, and hairstyles. Edo life reflected its dramatic arts.

The Torii school founded by Torii Kiyonobu, laid the foundations of kabuki art in its designs for billboards and playbills. Book illustrations and single-sheet prints in *sumizuri-e*—black ink designs on white paper—by Kiyonobu, which depicted kabuki topics, began to appear shortly before 1700. Kiyomasu was a contemporary of Kiyonobu and was also a leading artist who executed kabuki print designs in a more delicate and refined manner.

The Torii school held sway over *shibai-e* for close to a century until eclipsed by a brilliant new artist of the time, Katsukawa Shunsho. Shunsho was famous for his paintings of beautiful ladies. At the same time he founded a new school of actor print design that dominated the field between 1770 and 1790. From his studio emerged an exceptional group of artists—Shunko, Shunei, and Shunro (who later became famous as Hokusai). While another talented artist of the day, Buncho (1726-c.1792) was credited with the innovation of *nigao-e*, or depicting an actor's facial features, it was actually Shunsho who capitalized on the idea and gave the greatest power and expressiveness to his actors. At around this same time the *okubi-e*, or large-head portraits with exaggerated facial expressions, also began to emerge from the Katsukawa school.

In the year 1794, the mysterious genius of kabuki portraiture, Sharaku, emerged upon the scene for a brief ten months and produced about 140 prints. His identity and life are still shrouded in mystery and embroiled in debate, but his prints are recognized as masterpieces in capturing not only the character being played but the personality of the individual actor as well.

In the late eighteenth and early nineteenth centuries, the most popular portraitist of kabuki actors was Toyokuni I, who founded the Utagawa school. He often portrayed climactic moments on stage, so that the viewer could identify not only with the actor and his role, but with a particular highlight of the drama.

Utagawa school descendents, Toyokuni III (Kunisada) and Kuniyoshi carried on the traditions, but by the late nineteenth century, Edo culture was in a decline and *shibai-e* had had its day.

Woodblock print, by Sharaku (1794–95). Kabuki theater portrait of Ichikawa Ebizo as Takemura Sadanoshin. Modern reproduction. 9.20 × 6 in.

LANDSCAPE PRINTS—FUKEI-GA

WOODBLOCK PRINTS featuring landscapes arrived very late on the *ukiyo-e* scene, primarily in the nineteenth century. While some landscapes had been used as backgrounds for figure paintings by earlier artists, it was the founder of the leading school of the late eighteenth and early nineteenth centuries, Utagawa Toyoharu (1735-1814) who introduced Western perspective techniques into paintings of beauties and landscapes. Another Utagawa artist, Kuniyoshi, gained some recognition by bringing a fresh new concept to these techniques a short time later. However, the two artists who created an entirely new perception of landscapes and became the undisputed masters of *ukiyo-e* landscape prints were Katsushika Hokusai and Ando Hiroshige.

Hokusai (1760-1849) was a great painter who had originally studied under Shunsho. He continued his studies of all the other major schools on his own and eventually synthesized his own dynamic, and often eclectic, style. His "Thirty-Six Views of Mt. Fuji" is probably his most famous landscape series.

Due to the several processes necessary in woodblock printing and the fact that they were done by different artisans, the final woodblock print was not always true to the artist's original concept. However, Hokusai insisted on his own ideas taking precedence.

He was a loner, a complete individualist, constantly engrossed in his work and extremely prolific, painting right up until the time of his death at the age of ninety.

Hiroshige's prints (1797-1858) were the antithesis of Hokusai's. They were closer to true reflections of nature, subdued, poetic, and harboring a somewhat plaintive quality. While Hokusai used strong lines to conquer and capture a vital element in nature, with the viewer looking on from outside, Hiroshige used blocks of color coordinated with simplicity in design to harmonize with nature and bring the viewer as a participant into the picture.

Hiroshige's personal life was a sad one. Orphaned in early life, in his middle years he lost his first wife and only son. It is speculated that the depth of expression achieved by Hiroshige in his work, and the quiet, soothing, almost lonely beauty of many of his prints were a reflection of the emotions caused by these personal trials.

Woodblock print, by Hiroshige (1797–1858). Views of Edo. Spring Rain at
Nihonbashi. 1832. Approx. 14 × 10 in.

PRINTS OF BEAUTIFUL WOMEN—BIJINGA

THE ART OF BIJINGA, prints of beautiful women, had its origins in the colorful life of old Edo (modern Tokyo).

The city supported a sizeable group of transients, including the vast retinue of the various daimyo, workmen involved in building the city supplied from numerous regions by the daimyo, merchants from Osaka and Nagoya busily opening branch shops in the bustling city, and craftsmen supplying the expanding needs of the growing metropolis.

The two main pleasure pursuits of the day were the kabuki theater and the pleasure quarters, especially the Yoshiwara. Inside this licensed quarter, the rigid social code was dropped—any man could be king as long as he had money and the wit to use it. The pleasures—food, wine, entertainment, and women—were all available on a sliding scale that could accommodate even the pocketbook of an adventurous apprentice, not to mention the superior treatment afforded a wealthy merchant.

The *tayu*, or high-ranking courtesan, was the reigning queen, although only a handful achieved this exalted rank. As the most alluring symbol of womanhood, she was talked about and vied for, and it was she and her sisters that the woodblock print artists of the day most often depicted.

Moronobu and the early Torii school produced some prints of standing courtesans, and Choshun (1673–1753) and Kaigetsudo Ando were early *ukiyo-e* artists who contributed much to the image of female beauty.

The first woodblock artist to present a new image of femininity, soft, frail and youthfully sweet, was Suzuki Harunobu (1725–70). His portraits were not always of courtesans, however, but extended themselves to other famous beauties, including shopkeepers' wives and daughters.

The three artists considered master designers of *bijinga* are Torii Kiyonaga (1752–1815), Utamaro (1753–1806), and to a slightly lesser extent Chobunsai Eishi (1756–1829).

Kiyonaga produced a tall, stately image that became the prototype for artistic renditions of female beauty of that time.

Utamaro's prints featured exotically beautiful women and introduced new formats and composition—the large-head portraits and three-quarter prints against solid color backgrounds.

Eishi was the son of a samurai family and had a pure, delicate, refined style.

In the late Edo period, the Utagawa school led in depicting beautiful women and kabuki actors. However, two other independent artists, influenced by Utamaro's style, emerged: Eisen, who produced sensuous designs of courtesans, and Eizan, who faithfully followed Utamaro's concepts.

Woodblock print, by Utamaro (1753–1806). Two courtesans. Circa 1800. Approx. 14.5 × 10 in.

WRESTLER PRINTS—SUMO-E

SUMO-E, WOODBLOCK PRINTS of sumo subjects, gained popularity at the end of the eighteenth century when the matches became the craze of the day. They continued to be made into the Meiji period (1868-1911).

The sport of wrestling goes back as far as Japanese mythology, but the first recorded sumo matches were rituals dedicated to the gods with prayers for a bountiful harvest. These were performed within shrine precincts with other sacred dances and dramas in the Nara period (645-794).

The foundations of modern sumo were laid with professional groups organized during the colorful Edo period (1614-1868) to entertain the newly rising middle class. It was at this time that it became the national sport of Japan, and the present Japan Sumo Association came from these roots.

Subject matter of sumo prints includes portraits of well-known wrestlers, both in formal kimono and in their ceremonial aprons called *kesho-mawashi*; wrestling scenes; "entering the ring" ceremony scenes; bird's-eye-views of the sumo ring and spectators; and miscellaneous other scenes including sumo wrestlers partying.

Prints of grand champions, *yokozunas*, are popular among collectors, but not too plentiful. In the past three hundred years since the title was created, there have been only forty-six wrestlers who have won this honor.

In collecting sumo prints, the important points to consider are the quality of the art, the condition of the print, the subject matter, and the artist. These factors will set the price.

The artists best known for depicting sumo wrestlers are Shunei, Shunsho, Toyokuni I, Toyokuni III (Kunisada), and Kuniyoshi, but there are many more.

The earlier Edo prints are more desirable than the later Meiji ones, not just because of age, but because the Meiji colors became bright and garish in contrast to the softer, more subtle Edo tones.

It is advisable to specialize when forming a collection. The beginner is well advised to select one topic, one artist, or one popular wrestler and restrict his collecting to prints within this category. In this way a more comprehensive collection can be formed without a major financial investment. However, if generalized collecting is done at first, with an eye for the bargains, the collection can always be upgraded at a later date by trading and selling.

Either old or new ranking lists, called *banzuke*, issued after each tournament, should not be overlooked. Framed, they make delightful abstract art for modern settings and cost very little.

Woodblock print, by Toyokuni II (1802–1845?). Formal portrait of wrestler Sakaigawa. Approx. 14 × 10 in.

NAGASAKI AND YOKOHAMA PRINTS—
NAGASAKI-E, YOKOHAMA-E

NAGASAKI WOODBLOCK PRINTS were the rather crude product of *machi-e-shi*, unknown town artists. These prints flourished from the 1740s until around 1860.

From the middle 1600s Japan had been closed to the outside world with only the Dutch and Chinese allowed to remain at Nagasaki. The Chinese had a separate settlement on the mainland, but the Dutch were restricted to the tiny islet of Deshima in Nagasaki harbor. Many foreign ships came to call at port but, their petitions for trade with cloistered Japan having been rejected, they soon left.

The Dutch in Nagasaki offered the Japanese their only open window to the outside world and gave them a glimpse of the times through foreign books, pictures, maps, and medical publications.

Japanese tourists often visited scenic Nagasaki, eager to see anything connected with the exotic foreigners. Locally produced woodblock prints became popular souvenirs. Various nationalities—Dutch, Chinese, American, Russian, Korean, British—and their costumes were depicted. The inspiration for many probably came from book illustrations colored by the artists' imagination: foreign women, for example, were not allowed in Japan, yet were often pictured. Ships, boats, maps, and strange animals were favorite subjects, and especially foreigners indulging in simple pleasures such as eating and drinking, reading, writing, strolling, and hunting. Considering that the gun was little known, chairs were an oddity, and even a simple drinking glass was a curiosity, it is easy to see why the Japanese found these somewhat wooden Nagasaki prints entertaining.

In 1854, American Admiral Perry finally succeeded in signing a trade treaty with Japan that opened up the sequestered country. Four years later, commercial treaties were also effected with Russia, England, France, and the Netherlands. Yokohama was designated as the official port to handle the country's new commercial relations.

Yokohama-e, pictures depicting life in and around the foreign settlement of Yokohama, are generally believed to have been produced from about 1860 to 1880, although some scholars feel that the prints were only in production for a short six- or seven-year span.

In contrast to the Nagasaki prints, made by unskilled local artists, those of Yokohama were made mainly in Tokyo by members of the Utagawa school of *ukiyo-e*, the most notable of whom was Sadahide. Even so, *Yokohama-e* do not pretend to compete in artistic merit with prints of the traditional *ukiyo-e* school. Instead, they are a fascinating historical commentary on the early influx of foreigners to Japan.

Woodblock print, artist unknown. Chinese, Korean, Ryukyuan, Dutch, and Russian gentlemen. Circa 1830. 12.6 × 8.75 in.

SIX ANCIENT KILNS POTTERY—BIZEN, TAMBA, SETO, SHIGARAKI, ECHIZEN, TOKONAME

POTTERY MAKING BEGAN in Japan in the Neolithic period, called Jomon. The earliest forms were pots with pointed or rounded bottoms used for cooking, and the oldest of these is believed to be around twelve thousand years old.

While some pieces from the so-called Six Ancient Kilns date from the late Nara and early Heian periods (circa 800), they established their reputations for pottery late in the Kamakura period (1185-1333) by preserving and passing on to modern generations the ancient styles and techniques. Their first production was mainly large grain storage jars (with the exception of Seto), and these still remain some of Japan's most magnificent pottery. In the Momoyama period (1573-1614) there arose a great demand (continuing up to the present) for tea ceremony utensils, and the unassuming rustic simplicity of the wares from these kilns was perfect for this ritual.

Of the six kilns, Seto was by far the largest producing area and remains so today. The earliest glazed pottery came from Seto, influenced by contacts with China during the late Sung and Yüan dynasties (1127-1367).

Tokoname is close to Seto, and unfortunately for art lovers, its modern production is mainly brick, tile, and sewer pipe. However, there is a good ceramics museum in the city where fine examples of its past grandeur can be viewed.

Tamba is a mountainous province in the center of Japan, and the village kilns of this region took the name for their products. Only one village makes pottery today. The first pottery to have characteristics unique to the region was produced in the Kamakura period.

Old Tamba pottery is endowed with rich, erratic surfaces varying in both texture and color. This was caused partially by ashes from the burned wood in the kiln causing a natural ash glaze on the shoulders of the vessels.

Echizen, like Tamba, was another country kiln area that produced pottery mainly for local markets. Unlike Tamba, the kilns died out more than two hundred years ago, but the old pieces can be spectacular.

Shigaraki is a hill town near Kyoto that has been a pottery producing area since antiquity. Its wares can often be distinguished by small white granular spots in the finished pots due to impurities in the clay, and jars produced there often have simple incised designs scratched in a band around the shoulders.

Bizen is one of the ancient kiln sites still very active. Its older wares are most distinctive and highly prized by modern collectors. Bizen ware's natural ash glazes come in colors from red to black. Often there are patterns on the surface caused by straw or other materials adhering to the pot during firing.

The products of most of the kilns were originally just for farm use, but as devotees of the tea ceremony began to convert them to their own purposes, special tea ceremony utensils came to be made by most of the kilns.

Tokoname storage jar. Stoneware with natural ash glaze. Late eleventh century. H. 13 in.

BLACK SHIP, HOLLANDER PORCELAIN—
GOSO-SEN-DE

IN THE EARLY PART of the Edo era in Japan (from 1623-51), in order to consolidate the regime, a policy of isolation was adopted. The Japanese people were shut in, while all the foreigners were expelled. The only ones allowed to remain were the Dutch and Chinese, and the former were ordered to move from Hirado to the tiny artificial islet of Deshima in the harbor of Nagasaki.

During these years of isolation, the Dutch contributed much to the Japanese in keeping them apprised of progress in the outside world. They were Japan's only trading partners and furnished information from abroad, especially regarding the fields of medicine, global geography, military science, naval techniques, and Western art.

It was natural therefore, that one of the typical subjects for ceramic export ware was the Hollander and his "black ship." While the Imari kilns seem to have been the first to produce this ware, the Kutani kilns soon copied the patterns.

Porcelain production in Japan had begun early in the seventeenth century, and even though the laws forbidding trade with Europeans was vigorously enforced, some porcelains were smuggled out of the country via Chinese traders, and a few were sold in the Dutch East Indies and India through licensed Dutch traders. By the year 1664, the situation had changed, and it is recorded that one Dutch ship cargo of 45,000 pieces of Imari porcelain was sent directly to Holland.

Almost from the beginning of the Japanese porcelain export trade, there were two types of ceramic wares: those made for export and those made for use at home. Export wares consisted of matched sets of table China, decorated flower vases in pairs, and true Japanese dishes modified in size and shape to suit the needs of foreign buyers. Special orders depicting European patterns sent to Japan to be copied were also produced.

The "black ship" pattern, literally *goso-sen-de* ("five boats" decoration), pictures a typical Dutch vessel and Hollanders dressed in the frock coats and hats fashionable in Europe at the time. A piece with this pattern is a rare find in Japan today. Since it was principally an export pattern, it is likely that it might be found more readily in other countries.

Plate. Colored Imari porcelain with black ship, Hollander design. Modern reproduction. D. 10 in.

BLUE-AND-WHITE PORCELAINS—SOMETSUKE

The beginning of porcelain with cobalt blue underglaze decoration in China is still controversial. Traditionally the earliest blue-and-white ware is assigned to the Yüan dynasty, but there is evidence now to think it started in the Sung dynasty. It was first introduced into Korea during the early Yi dynasty (around 1443). The techniques came to Japan by way of Korea in the early 1600s.

When the Japanese general Toyotomi Hideyoshi failed in his Korean expedition and after his death, the Japanese departed Korea and brought with them back to Japan a great number of Korean potters. This led to a rapid expansion of the ceramic industry in Japan.

Around 1616, a Korean potter by the name of Ri Sanpei is credited with discovering the precious clay, called kaolin, necessary to make porcelain. The discovery of kaolin revolutionized the ceramic industry in Japan, and within fifty years many of the kilns had changed from pottery to porcelain manufacturing.

Blue-and-white cobalt underglaze wares in Japan are called *sometsuke*, meaning "dyed" or "printed." The blue is produced by cobalt pigments painted onto the biscuit, after which the entire piece is glazed and fired.

The shades of blue vary greatly from a soft, gray blue to a strong blue with flecks of black where the pigment has settled, or a clear, sapphire blue associated with the famous Ming blue-and-white.

Early Japanese blue-and-white followed Korean and Chinese models closely in both patterns and shapes, although the Chinese wares were much more refined in body, glaze, and color.

Eventually, however, the designs became Japanized, and the quality reached a very high standard. Even though overglaze colored enamels became popular from the end of the seventeenth century, there was still a demand for blue-and-white patterns, and they continue to be produced today.

Beautiful porcelain is a pleasure to use, and most shapes are easily adaptable to modern use. If a dinner set is beyond reach, this should not discourage the random collector from seeking odd pieces to be used as sauce dishes, soup cups, ashtrays, nut and canapé dishes, or as serving pieces with a set of undecorated modern china.

Plate and cup. Blue-and-white Imari porcelain. Late nineteenth century. Plate D. 8.25 in., cup H. 2.25 in.

Bowl. Blue-and-white Imari porcelain. Eighteenth century. H. 5.5 in.

EXPORT PORCELAINS

JAPANESE PORCELAIN PRODUCTION began in the Arita district of Kyushu in the early seventeenth century, after the discovery of white porcelain clay (kaolin) by a Korean potter, Ri Sampei.

Recent findings seem to verify another line of porcelain development at about the same time or a little earlier (circa 1600) by Chinese potters brought from the mainland to Japan. Porcelain shards from some old Arita kilns show that Ming type greenish celadons with molded designs and Sung style bluish celadons with incised decoration were being produced.

Chinese and Korean porcelain had long been collected and held in high esteem by the Japanese, so the discovery of kaolin caused many kilns to change quickly from pottery to porcelain production.

It is interesting to note that three of the earliest porcelains, Kakiemon, Imari, and Nabeshima were all produced very near each other in the Arita district. Yet they are vastly different in design. This may reflect, in addition to artistic talents, the great secrecy that surrounded the industry in its formative years. Production formulas, colors, and designs were held closely within the confines of each kiln and jealously guarded. It was to little avail, since the industry spread rapidly.

The overseas trade in Arita porcelains began around the middle of the seventeenth century, when the industry was still in its infancy. It was fortunate for the Japanese that at that time Chinese porcelains, which enjoyed great popularity in both Asia and Europe, fell into a period when export was almost completely suspended. This was due to internal problems of the new Ch'ing regime. The Dutch East India Company turned to Japan to fill their European orders, and consequently the Japanese export volume rose dramatically. In fact, Japanese porcelain patterns soon came into such vogue that they were copied by both European and Chinese kilns.

In the seventeenth and eighteenth centuries and until the Meiji period, most of the Japanese porcelains were of high quality. With the Meiji Restoration however, the Arita kilns, among others, began to produce "Nagasaki wares." These export wares in European shapes were generally decorated with a rather poor quality of Imari overglaze red and gold.

Plate. Blue-and-white export porcelain with bird and flower design. Eighteenth century. D. 17.75 in.

IMARI PORCELAINS

IMARI PORCELAIN production began early in the seventeenth century in the Arita district on the island of Kyushu.

By the second half of the century, Japanese porcelains were already being exported by the Dutch. The Arita ware was called Imari in Europe, after the name of the port from which it was exported. It was so successful on the continent that the Chinese kilns at Ching-te-chen began to imitate many of the Japanese patterns.

Nabeshima and Kakiemon porcelains, also from Arita, were called by their family and fief names, since they developed designs and qualities distinctly their own.

The oldest Japanese porcelain is called *shoki-imari*, "earliest Imari." It was produced from around 1600–50. Among these early wares were a celadon color, an underglaze sky blue, and an iron and underglaze blue on white.

The term *ko-Imari*, or "old Imari," is used to identify porcelains made from about 1650–1750. Around this time the first overglaze red enamel was produced. The overglaze, colored enamel wares joined the other types made previously and became wildly popular.

Some of the colored Imari was called *nishiki-de*, or "brocade wares," since the decoration generally covered every inch of the pieces.

Many of the Arita porcelains were made for export. However, the bulk was made for use in Japan, and the designs reflect the ornate taste of the Edo period (1614–1868). This is also evident in gold and inlaid lacquer ware and shimmering golden screens of this same era.

The designs and workmanship of Arita porcelains were of fine quality. It was not until the nineteenth century that their quality declined, the colors becoming gaudy and the designs overworked.

Imari porcelains in colored enamels and blue-and-white are still being made today, and many are of excellent quality. Both new and antique Imari enjoy such a following that prices continue to soar.

Japanese shapes are easily adapted to Western uses. The covered rice bowl becomes a candy dish or sugar bowl, the slim, covered soup bowl a cigarette container, and the small round pickle dishes are perfect ash trays. For those with a sizeable budget, a set of dinner plates can be a conversation piece and a joy forever on a special dinner table.

Bowl. Colored Imari porcelain. Early nineteenth century. H. 7 in.

KAKIEMON PORCELAIN

KAKIEMON IS CONSIDERED one of the finest of Japanese porcelains. Bright, clear enamel colors and elegant brushwork are two of the major characteristics of this highly refined ware.

Kakiemon I, whose name was originally Kizaemon Sakaida, is traditionally credited with producing the first Japanese overglaze, colored enamels. However, this is under investigation by modern scholars. He was born on the outskirts of Arita, a small town near the port city of Nagasaki. This region of Kyushu was a great pottery-producing area and also the place where Chinese ceramics first entered the country.

It was the beginning of the colorful seventeenth century, the Japanese porcelain industry was in its infancy and only producing blue-and-white and celadon wares, and Kizaemon, who worked in the kilns from an early age, devoted years to perfecting the technique of *aka-e*, or red overglaze enamel ware, which was highly developed in China. A friend had purchased the precious secrets of the process from a Chinese potter in Nagasaki, and they worked together to perfect the formula. After many failures, they finally succeeded and Kizaemon presented an alcove decoration of a red persimmon with the new glaze to the local feudal lord. The lord was so delighted he immediately ordered Kizaemon to change his name to Kakiemon, *kaki* meaning persimmon and also the brilliant new red color they had produced.

The Kakiemon kilns produced three types of designs. One was based on Chinese designs of the Ming and early Ch'ing dynasties; the second was a simple, naturalistic Japanese design based on trees, flowers, animals, birds, and landscapes, and the third was a European-style design influenced by the Dutch.

Kakiemon porcelains are highly refined, the body a very pure white, and the colors brilliant and clear. Unlike the highly decorated Imari porcelains, there is great restraint in the delicate designs. They seldom cover more than one-third to one-half the surface of the object.

When Kakiemon porcelains were exported to Europe in the late 1600s, they immediately won acclaim, and the factories of Delft in Holland, Meissen in Germany, and Worcester in England began to copy the Kakiemon patterns.

Since the time of Kakiemon I, the eldest son of the Sakaida family has taken this illustrious name, and the thirteenth generation is presently carrying on the traditions of this famous Japanese kiln.

Old Kakiemon porcelain is very costly. However, designs in the Kakiemon style were done by many other kilns, and some pieces of this type can still be found at moderate prices. New Kakiemon is expensive, but not exhorbitant, considering the high quality and workmanship lavished on the modern ware.

Plate. Early Kakiemon blue-and-white porcelain with fish. Circa 1680. D. 7.6 in.

KUTANI WARE

Ko-Kutani ("old Kutani") is a porcelaneous ware believed to have been produced in Japan for only a short period of time from around 1655 to 1703 although the actual dates are far from clear.

Kaga Province, the home of Kutani village, faces the Japan Sea. In the Edo period, Kaga was the domain of the powerful and extremely wealthy Maeda clan of feudal lords. Kaga was not only a major center of agriculture, but also was important in the Japan Sea shipping trade. Due to this, the prosperous populace enjoyed a high degree of culture, and the demand for luxury goods such as porcelain was strong. The late Ming and early Ch'ing overglazed enamel wares were especially popular.

Therefore, when word of the Arita success in producing overglaze porcelains reached Lord Maeda Toshiharu, he immediately sent one of his retainers off to Kyushu as an industrial spy. The man returned ten years later, and the Kutani kilns were established and began to manufacture their own decorated porcelains.

The *ko-Kutani* porcelains differed from the Arita in their much larger and more unconventional shapes, which expressed a highly individual artistic interpretation. Also the color palette is much darker and bolder with red, indigo, vivid green, dark purple, egg yellow, and chocolate brown predominant.

In the *ao-Kutani*, or "green Kutani," the entire body is covered on both sides in a deep green glaze and decorated with strong simple designs such as fruit, birds and flowers, fans, and brocade motifs. In addition to this *ko-Kutani* decorated in the Japanese style, other designs were in imitation of Chinese wares, while still others followed the styles of Imari and Kakiemon.

Ko-Kutani ware has no seal, and the name Kutani did not appear until after 1876. Except for the earliest pieces, many of the older ornamental pieces bear the character *fuku*, "happiness." Later the characters for Kutani were written in characters with a brush, and still later the name of the artist was added.

It is speculated that Kutani bodies were not always made at the kiln site but some were done elsewhere and brought to Kutani to be decorated. Modern research is expected to clarify this soon.

The Kutani kilns remained idle from the early eighteenth to the early nineteenth century, when they were revived briefly by Aoki Mokubei of Kyoto, but did not necessarily use the old Kutani patterns and shapes. A few years later, circa 1824, they were reorganized by the Yoshidaya family, who rekindled the traditions of the original kilns in design motifs and colors. This reorganization has lasted into modern times.

Plate. Colored Kutani porcelain from the Yoshidaya kilns. Early twentieth century. D. 14.5 in.

NABESHIMA PORCELAIN

EARLY NABESHIMA WARE is considered to be technically the finest porcelain ever produced in Japan.

Lord Nabeshima, the feudal ruler of Saga Province, founded the kilns around 1598 upon his return from the Korean expedition. With him he brought several hundred Korean potters, who began to produce wares for the personal use of his family. These potters were treated as members of the household. Their work was considered so important that the talented were often raised to the exalted status of samurai.

The finest pieces were given as gifts to friends and government officials, and up to ninety percent of the production of the kilns was destroyed in order to assure the finest quality.

A few select kilns, including Nabeshima and Hirado, were called *oniwa-gama*, "garden kilns," since they were often located in the garden of the lord and under his strict control.

It was a time of great intrigue, and many risked their lives to learn formulas for new glazes or a different firing technique. The Nabeshima kilns were closely guarded and managed to keep their secrets until the Meiji period (1868-1912), when the wares were sold for the first time commercially and also imitated. By that time, the quality had deteriorated considerably.

Nabeshima ware is outstanding for its beauty and the originality of its boldly painted designs. One of the characteristics of Nabeshima ware is that fifty percent or more of the space is covered by the design. The motifs are large and pictorial in concept, with a soft and refined finish. They appear very modern even today. The types of wares produced by these porcelain kilns were celadons, blue-and-white, pure white, and colored enamels over white. Subjects included fruits and vegetables, waves, flowers, and scroll or ribbon designs. A particular favorite was the low zigzag fence.

Other distinguishing features are their "comb pattern" foot rim and either the Chinese coin design or chrysanthemums and leaves painted on the outside rim of the dish.

Old Nabeshima ware is in a price range that restricts it to a few collectors. Modern Nabeshima remains expensive, since the old traditions are still carried on by the Imaemon family, the original potters of this famous ware. Meiji and Taisho era copies of Nabeshima patterns from the Arita and Kaga kilns are plentiful and comparatively low in both quality and price.

Plate. Colored Nabeshima porcelain with peony design. Seventeenth century. D. 8 in.

FURNITURE

JAPAN IS ONE OF THE few civilizations that did not develop its own specialized furniture forms. Actually, little was required.

Tatami mats made of *igusa* (rush) covered the floors and were used for sitting. Cloth cushions and armrests provided a note of comfort by day, and padded bedding was unrolled for sleeping. In the sparsely furnished rooms of the castles and in the mansions of the nobility, fine art, consisting of paintings on screens, hanging scrolls, and sliding doors, provided a focal point indoors. Architecture played a special role both indoors and out, and the garden was an important element.

In common households the room with the *irori*, or open-pit hearth, was the center of activity. Low trays, *bon*, and table trays, *sanbo*, were utilized in serving. They were portable and always removed after the refreshments had been served, preserving the tranquil setting. Folding screens were used to ward off drafts. Desks, tables, and stands for religious and cultural pursuits were also developed, mainly from imported prototypes.

Buddhism, introduced in the sixth century, brought with it new interior furnishings. Japan began to assimilate and produce certain styles of long- and short-legged altar tables and benches on which to place offerings of food and flowers. Squatty cabinets and bookcases in which to store the precious Buddhist sutras were built. Raised platforms with ornamental cutouts around the four sides were for sitting. The Chinese folding and straight-back chairs came into limited use among the heirarchy of the temples as well as for members of the nobility and samurai classes when traveling.

The clothing stand, *iko*, was brought from China and adopted by the Japanese, although surprisingly, the Chinese chairs, benches, and beds were rejected on a popular level in favor of living on tatami matting.

Chests of drawers, *tansu*, originally imported from Korea, came into household use at a much later date (circa 1600). Before that time, large boxes with lids and rectangular chests were used for clothes storage, and smaller boxes of varied size and shape for containing personal items.

Since furniture was never produced in great quantity in Japan, (except for the later chests), the objects are usually finished in some special way. Many pieces are lacquered and might have inlay or gold lacquer decoration. Other pieces have unusual and artistic metalwork, while still others are designed to enhance the natural woods from which they are fashioned.

Altar table. Wood. Early nineteenth century. H. 9 in., L. 24 in.

Folding chair. Polychromed, gilded wood and leather. Early nineteenth century. H. 3.5 ft.

INCENSE BURNERS—KORO

IN JAPAN, INCENSE BURNING came into popularity along with the new rites of Buddhism imported in the sixth century. It was also quickly taken up by those Shinto sects that incorporated many of the new Buddhist rituals into their own ceremonies.

In China, the "hill-censer," an incense stove, originated during the Han dynasty (206 B.C.-220 A.D.).

Ancient Chinese rituals included the burning of southernwood and mugwort, but it was not until the reign of the Han Emperor Wu (140-87 B.C.) that, due to his expansionist policies in politics and trade, Parthian incense and attar of roses were imported from Central Asia.

Undoubtedly these new imported aromatics caused a flurry among the metalworkers and potters of the day to find a unique and suitable form in which to burn them.

The result was the *po shan lu*, or literally "brazier of the vast mountain," but often referred to as the "hill censer." The name was derived from the cover, which is in the shape of a hill with openings from which the perfumed fumes can escape. The top sits on a stemmed bowl similar in shape to a goblet, and the stem is connected to a base. Later Chinese incense burners were patterned after the ancient bronze sacrificial vessels of the Shang and Chou dynasties. The favorite form of this type of incense burner was taken from the *ting*, a cauldron on three legs used for preparing sacrificial food. So even in ancient times one can find old forms converted to new usages.

Today, the burning of incense is still practiced in Japan, especially in connection with religious rites and veneration for the dead.

Antique incense burners, both Japanese and Chinese, in porcelain, lacquer, and a variety of metals are available in a wide range of prices.

Soft green celadon incense burners are often seen in the three-legged *ting* style. Ones of blue-and-white porcelain are varishaped and many times accompanied by beautifully incised metal covers with flower and bird designs. Bronzes are seen in traditional shapes as well as in appealing animal forms.

People who spend time in the Orient often come to enjoy the soothing fragrance of incense burning and use *koro* for their original purpose.

They may also be converted to other uses. A small, porcelain incense burner, for example, would make an attractive sugar bowl or candy or cigarette dish, while a larger size might hold a flower arrangement or a plant.

Incense burner. Celadon porcelain duck with lid. Early nineteenth century. H. 4.5 in.

RED AND BLACK LACQUER—NEGORO

NEGORO LACQUERED ARTICLES are usually of cinnabar or coral-red color applied over a black lacquer undercoating. When new, these articles have no design, but through daily use and cleaning, the black undercoating in time shows through, creating aesthetically pleasing patterns. *Negoro* articles are strong, and usually the lacquer has been applied directly to a wooden base without the use of linen.

The origin of *negoro* ware dates from about 1288 A.D. At that time priests from Mount Koya, the center of Shingon Buddhism located south of Osaka, moved to Wakayama Prefecture to take charge of Negoro-dera, a monastery in that area. These priests made red and black lacquer eating and drinking vessels for themselves, and the name of the monastery became attached generally to plain red lacquer utensils. Most of the pieces of this sort are ordinary, practical shapes, but endowed with a feeling of great classicism and monumental beauty. *Negoro* ware is much admired by the Japanese for these understated qualities.

A famous story that illustrates the Japanese love for that which is subtle is told of the famous artist Ogata Korin, who was known for his eccentricities.

In his day, it was fashionable to go cherry blossom viewing at Arashiyama in Kyoto and to make some grand gesture on this occasion. On one such day, as his fellow picnicers unveiled their elaborately decorated lunchboxes, he took out a simple bamboo sheath, such as any poor man would have wrapped his rice balls in, and ate his lunch under the astonished gaze of his friends. When the food was gone, there appeared on the inside of the sheath an exquisitely lacquered picture of a landscape with figures. Korin, following the style of a common man, nonchalantly rolled it up and tossed it into the river.

Boxes, bowls and trays are among the items produced by the *negoro* technique. The older examples are rare and expensive. Many of the more recent pieces have been artificially worn to make the black show through. However, whether authentic or not, the combination of red and black lacquer in *negoro*-type objects is still very beautiful and decorative.

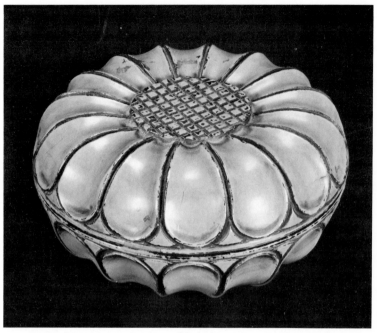

Covered bowl. *Negoro* (coral red over black) lacquer on wood. Nineteenth century. D. 7 in.

SUTRA BOXES—KYOBAKO

SUTRA BOXES, *kyobako*, are containers for the scroll writings of the Buddhist religion. These sutras are scriptural narratives, especially the dialogues of the Buddha.

According to traditional accounts, the official introduction of Buddhism occurred in 552 A.D. when the Korean king, Syong-mong presented the Japanese imperial family with a gilt-bronze statue of the Buddha, together with some sutras and implements of worship.

Prince Shotoku (592-628) became a great proponent of Buddhism and ordered the erection of numerous temples for promotion of the new faith. The oldest preserved copy of a Buddhist sutra was made by the Priest Horin in 687.

In the early days of Buddhism, court nobles, priests, and common Buddhist believers followed the custom of copying Buddhist sutras, which were then donated to temples as votive offerings—to show devotion, and for propagation of the Buddhist doctrine. Copying sutras is still done today by a small group of people, but more often as a spiritual exercise to put aside worries and troubles of worldly life.

During the Heian (794-1185) and Muromachi (1333-1573) periods, sutras were copied and buried. Many of the sutra boxes of those times were made of bronze or silver to better protect the writings from the dampness of the earth.

Preserved in the Shosoin Imperial Treasurehouse are two sutras with cases and covers, one of which bears an interesting inscription. In 741, it was ordered that a temple, with a seven-storied pagoda be built in every province of the realm, and this particular sutra be copied and placed in each pagoda.

When a civil war was suppressed in 764, the Empress Koken wished to express her joy and thanks by presenting sutras to Buddhist temples. She ordered the printing of one million sutras, each contained in a miniature wooden pagoda.

Antique sutra boxes are most often made of lacquered wood. Occasionally one in bronze or another metal may be found. Lovely storage boxes for a variety of items, they vary in size and shape but usually are similar to a large rectangular, oblong, or square jewelry case.

Sutra box. *Negoro,* (coral red over black) lacquer on wood. Fifteenth century.
H. 5.6 in., L. 14 in.

TEMPLE LANTERNS—TORO

BRONZE LANTERNS, *seido-toro*, were first used in temples and shrines in Japan where in early days all ceremonies were held at night.

Their use as an implement for Buddhist worship originated in India, and they were first brought to Japan through China in the Nara period (645–794).

At this time the native Japanese Shinto religion quickly took on many of the facets of Buddhism, blending them into their own rituals, and bronze lanterns also came to be used at Shinto shrines.

The oldest bronze lantern in Japan stands in front of the Todai-ji temple in Nara, which also houses the great Buddha. It is octagonal in shape, about fifteen feet tall, and has openwork panels depicting lions running amid clouds and Buddhist saints playing bamboo flutes.

During the ensuing Heian period (794–1185), the use of bronze lanterns was extended to the imperial court and residences of the nobles. At court the shape of the lanterns was square, like a house, and they were often made of iron. The nobles' lanterns followed the same shape but were more often of wood.

In later centuries it became fashionable to present bronze lanterns as votive offerings to shrines or temples to pray for military victories or special favors.

The Kasuga Shrine in Nara is famous for its one thousand hanging bronze lanterns as well as the more than two thousand stone lanterns lining the approach to the shrine. On the mystical nights of August 15 and February 3 all the lanterns are lit and ritual dances are performed. Countless flickering shadows fall among the giant trees and around the monumental architecture of the shrine and combine with the sounds of ancient musical instruments to create an otherworldly atmosphere—an experience that both visitors from abroad and Japanese never forget.

Antique bronze and iron lanterns used in modern settings are very decorative by day and at night offer soft, dancing patterns that modern lighting cannot duplicate.

Temple lantern. Bronze. Early eighteenth century. H. 24 in.

WINE POURERS—CHOSHI

THE JAPANESE WINE POURER, *choshi*, is a ceremonial wine holder used at shrines and temples for weddings and on other auspicious occasions.

It seems to have originated with the rites of the Shinto religion. From ancient times each family would brew their own saké and offer it to the gods on special occasions as well as share it with the community on festival days. *Kami* to the Japanese people is a term indicating an invisible force or power that controls the universe, human life, and personal happiness. It is closely related to nature. Offerings of food and wine to *kami* were often made to invoke favors or give thanks for wishes granted. They were also part of the ritual for important ceremonial occasions, such as special feast days and weddings.

In ceremonies, wine in early times was served in large, shallow pottery cups that were passed among the guests, each taking a sip from the same cup. Later lacquered wooden containers were made, some of which could hold up to a half-gallon of saké.

The communal drinking of saké has long been the most important part of the Japanese wedding ceremony, with the vows solemnized by the sharing of saké by the bride and groom. Until recently the ceremony took place in the home of either one of the prospective partners with no heavy religious associations. It is just since the turn of the century that weddings at shrines with Shinto rites came into popularity. Probably the church weddings of Japanese Christians in the Meiji era provided the impetus for this new trend. Buddhist temples, too, followed the example and began to offer marriage rites as part of their services.

After the ceremonial sipping of wine by the bride and groom, saké is then served to all the attendents, poured from the *choshi*, and a toast is offered to the new husband and wife for a happy and long life together.

Wine pourers are varied in size and usually finished in lustrous black or red lacquer or a combination of the two. They make attractive flower containers, can be used in their original way for serving a liquid refreshment, or make decorative food and fruit bowls.

Wine pourer. Black lacquer (red lacquer inside) on wood. Early nineteenth century. H. 6.5, D. 8.5 in.

WOODEN ARCHITECTURAL CARVINGS

IN JAPAN, SCULPTURAL ART is often seen in older temples, castles, and mansions. Transom partitions are called *ramma*. They are often decorated with latticework, open carvings of animals, birds, flowers, clouds, and subjects from religion and mythology. Placed horizontally between a ceiling and the upper groove of the sliding door frame, they allow air to circulate freely within the structure.

Carved elephant heads and other massive designs decorate the wooden beam ends on Buddhist temples. Carved "hanging fish," *gegyo*, found in the upper portion of the gable, were originally added as a charm against fire.

Sculptured designs in wood and metalwork have been a part of Japanese architecture in houses, shrines, and temples since early times. In contrast to the West, where the place of worship was distinctly different from the home, in Japan residential and temple construction was basically alike.

New architectural styles were imported from China in the sixth century along with Buddhism and exerted great influence on Japanese architecture from that time on. However, the native Shinto style—simple, pure, and dignified—retained its early form until the present time, with the Buddhist influx altering it only in small details.

In the Nara period (645–794), architectural design and accessories were simple, with many cloud forms, latticework, and line engravings on beams and brackets. From the Muromachi period (1333–1573) sculpture was used as architectural ornamentation. This new taste culminated in the Momoyama style (1573–1614), which consisted mainly of brightly colored sculptural designs, colored paintings on walls and doors, and ornate gilt metal fittings.

These were all developed to make the castles and mansions of the feudal lords and their retainers as beautiful and ostentatious as possible. Since there was no furniture as such used in the Japanese abode, it was only through architectural art forms that this could be accomplished.

Carvings and ornamentation from old temples and homes that have been demolished make charming and interesting three-dimensional art objects.

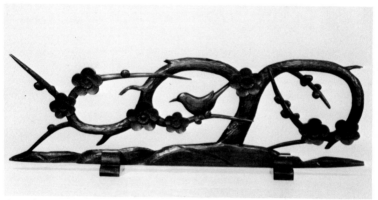

Carved transom (*ramma*). Wood. Early twentieth century. H. 6 in.

MENUKI

MENUKI ARE PAIRS of small metal ornaments, secured one to each side of the hilt of the Japanese sword by means of the braid that covers the hilt. They are functional, miniature works of art that portray a wide range of subjects in refined detail.

Their original purpose was to hold in place the peg that locks the blade and hilt together. Later their position was moved, and their purpose was to allow a better grip on the handle. From the late Kamakura period on, with the change in sword style, the *menuki* were placed on each side of the handle under the grasp of the fingers to prevent slipping.

The earliest known Japanese swords are of copper from the Yayoi culture (200 B.C.—200 A.D.). In the following Tumulus period (200–552), swords and fittings of other metals were made; many have cast handles featuring Chinese motifs, indicating an early cultural exchange.

During the Kamakura period (1185–1333), martial metalwork made great advances, not only in quality of technique, but also in ornamentation. The sword became the symbol of the warrior and the military government of the shogunate. It was in the following Muromachi period (1333–1573), when the sword was no longer hung from the belt but stuck into it, that new sword accessories appeared, among them *menuki*. During this period, a maker of sword ornaments by the name of Goto won recognition for his excellent craftsmanship, and his descendents continued this tradition until the early Meiji period.

In the peaceful Edo period (1614–1868), with increasing prosperity and the elimination of warfare, swords were still worn as a personal weapon, but greater energy went into the design and production of the sword accessories.

The Edo metal artisans often took their inspiration from the painters of the day, and subject matter ranged from historic and mythological tales and heroes to animals of all types and such natural subjects as flowers, trees, and birds, and even landscapes.

Menuki can be found in shops specializing in swords and sword accessories as well as in an occasional antique shop. Small, averaging. just over an inch wide, they can be useful as tie pins or cuff links.

Menuki mounted as cuff links. Plum blossoms in metal alloy. Late nineteenth century. L. 1.5 in.

SWORD GUARDS—TSUBA

THE JAPANESE SWORD GUARD, *tsuba*, is a heavy metal disc attached between the sword hilt and the blade. It is one of the most important parts of the Japanese sword.

The sword and its accessories were to the samurai what the rules and utensils of the tea ceremony are to the tea masters. They embodied the beliefs, principles, and status of their users in their design and function.

Metalwork in Japan can be traced back to the Yayoi culture (circa 200 B.C.–200 A.D.), and swords made of copper are one of the earliest examples. During the following periods and prior to 900 A.D., steel swords were produced, though not of good quality. During the middle Heian period (circa 900 A.D.) to the early Muromachi period (1450 A.D.), the samurai class came into existence and brought with it a golden age of Japanese swordsmiths.

The functions of the sword guard were primarily to protect the hand by preventing the opponent's sword from sliding forward, to act as a center of gravity and balance, and to keep the hilt away from the body. However, it has always been regarded as more important for its ornamental and philosophic rather than its functional value. When the samurai wore his sword, the guard would come almost at the center of his body and was associated with the dignity of his appearance. It portrayed not only his class distinction, but the pattern etched, carved, cut, or inlaid into the metal was symbolic of the ideas, aesthetics, and emotions of its owner. In fact, the *tsuba* was such a precious thing to the samurai, it is doubtful if he would ever allow his opponent's blade to come near it. On the other hand, the opponent would hardly wish to strike a *tsuba* with his own keen sword edge, which was painstakingly produced and always carefully guarded.

Tsuba usually have patterns on both sides and one or two extra holes to permit insertion of a utility knife, *kozuka*, skewer, *kogai*, or split chopsticks, *waribashi*. The *kogai* was the samurai's personal utensil. He used it as a hair-arranging stick, and it also has a handy extension at one end for cleaning the ears.

In 1871, among the reformations of the Meiji period, an edict was issued preventing the wearing of swords. This brought the production of swords and their accessories to a quiet end, except as art objects.

Sword guards are miniature works of art that can be enjoyed purely for their sculptural beauty or still function in new ways. They make handsome desk accessories as paperweights and can be dramatic conversation pieces when worn as pendants.

Sword guard. Iron openwork. Early eighteenth century. D. 3 in.

Sword guard. Iron with figures of foreigner and other designs in inlaid gold. Eighteenth century. D. 2.8 in.

BOOKS—HON

THE TOOLS OF BOOK-MAKING were first brought to Japan in 610 A.D. by a Korean monk named Doncho, who was knowledgeable in the production of paper, inks, and colors. He was also a scholar and knew the five books of the Chinese classics.

The best collection of Japan's oldest specimen of printing is in the Horyu-ji temple in Nara. This is a Buddhist scripture printed by woodblock and inserted in the core of minature wooden pagodas in 764. This scripture was once thought to be the oldest example of printing in the world, but a somewhat older printed scripture was found in Korea. One million copies of the Japanese sutra were printed, a formidible production even today.

Early Japanese books were printed entirely from woodblocks. Popular subjects for illustration were the *Tales of Genji*, poetry and novels, dramatic scenes from the kabuki theater, and instructional, and cultural texts on such subjects as flower arranging and tea ceremony, and even artists' manuals. Black and white drawings were often highlighted with color washes and paints applied by hand.

Printing received great stimulus during the Edo period (1614–1868), when the first books for mass distribution were made. Although the Korean movable type was used on an experimental basis for forty years and European movable type, imported by missionaries circa 1600, was used for a few government documents and books, the woodblock method continued in general use until the early Meiji period.

In woodblock printing, the text was first pasted, face down, on a slab of wood. Then the paper was oiled so that the writing or illustration could be clearly seen. The engraver then carved out the spaces around the lines, leaving the text in relief. The block was inked, a sheet of paper layed on, and this was pressed against the block with a thick pad. Since the paper was highly absorbent, printing was done on one side only. The printed sheets were folded to form pages and then bound.

During Edo times, the general populace was eager for the education and entertainment offered by books, although not everyone could afford to purchase them. Special book-lending shops called *kashihon-ya* offered light fiction, children's books, and even magazines to shop employees, geishas, and artisans at a very low fee. These book lenders were in part responsible for the high literacy rate Japan achieved in a relatively short period of time. They still do a bustling business in rural Japanese communities today.

Japan's secondhand bookshops are exciting depositories of antique books and pictures. In Tokyo, try the area called Jimbocho, where you will find one shop after another. Old and used books on Oriental arts and antiques (some in English) can also be found there.

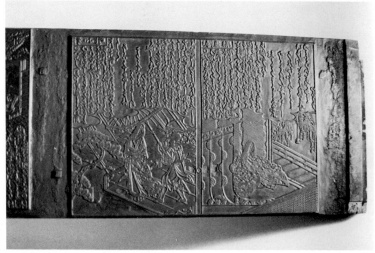

Woodblock for printing an illustrated book (*e-hon*). Early nineteenth century. H. 8.5 in.

CALLIGRAPHY—SHO

THE GREEKS CALLED IT *kalligraphia*, the Chinese words are *shu-fa*, and the Japanese imported it and named it *sho*. It means beautiful writing or calligraphy.

The earliest form of writing in the Far East is found on the oracle bones of the Shang dynasty (1523–1028 B.C.), bone fragments containing records of questions asked by those ancient peoples to their ancestors and gods. It is a miracle that these bones have been preserved, for early in this century they were first dug up by farmers who sold them as "dragon bones" to be used as medicine for a number of ills. Luckily, many were rescued from this fate. The Chou dynasty brought many inscriptions on bronze ritual vessels and bamboo strips. Rolls of silk were used for record keeping until the Chinese invention of paper during the Han dynasty, reportedly in 105 A.D.

Legibility and precision, the attributes of Western penmanship have little relationship to the brush writing of the East. The essence of calligraphy is not in the written word but in the expression of life into each written character, an inner rhythm seeking expression through brush and paper.

Japan inherited its early calligraphic content and styles from China, and in the Nara period (645–794) this consisted chiefly of the copying of Buddhist sutras and ancient Chinese literature by scholar-priests and members of the imperial household. In the following Heian era (794–1185), when Japan was isolated from China, a true Japanese form of painting was born, and calligraphy, too, came to reflect a native flavor.

The influx of Zen Buddhism into Japan from China beginning in the Kamakura period (1185–1333) added a strong religious emphasis to the calligraphic arts once again, and the writings were often coupled with *sumi-e*—ink paintings—in black and white.

Calligraphy provides an interesting, vibrant abstract art form to nonreaders of Chinese characters. It also lends itself to modern settings.

The calligraphy on one of my favorite scrolls, purchased for a mere pittance, leaps out at the viewer in its strength and vigor. It was done fifty years ago by a gentleman of ninety-three. The deep, black ink sings from the mellowed paper, "the spirit of God is within me."

The viewer instinctively senses that special moment when the brush touched paper and shares a supreme experience.

Even today there are many hanging scrolls of calligraphy, sometimes coupled with paintings, inexpensively available.

Calligraphy of the character "dream" and butterflies. Ink and soft color on paper. Mid nineteenth century. 18 × 11 in.

LETTER BOXES—FUBAKO

THE JAPANESE LETTER BOX, *fubako*, came into use in Japan almost four hundred years ago.

Tokugawa Ieyasu established his ruling shogunate at Edo, modern Tokyo, in 1603, ushering in a period when the country would know great unity and the arts would flourish.

Ieyasu realized that communications were essential to holding the provincial daimyo in hand, and so an elaborate network for carrying messages was established. Also this clever shogun required the daimyo to be in residence in the capitol every alternate year. In the years they were allowed to return to their provincial homes, their families were required to remain in Edo. It was a refined and effective way of holding hostages.

It is easy to imagine that with the regional rulers separated first from their fiefs and sources of revenue and then from the political intrigues of the capitol and their families, it was essential that a great many letters and documents be exchanged.

The letter box became an integral part of this life and carried many important missives back and forth. Naturally, love letters also were exchanged in this manner.

Fubako are usually finished in rich black or brown lacquers with patterns in gold, silver, and occasionally other colors. Gold lacquer ware, *maki-e*, came into popularity in the late seventeenth century and has remained the most elegant and expensive of all the lacquer techniques to the present day.

Although letter boxes have outlived their original purpose, they make unusual and decorative candy or cigarette boxes, with or without their corded tie. On many the ties have become worn and have been discarded. The price range is wide, depending upon the age, quality of the lacquer, and workmanship.

Letter box. Black lacquer on wood with gold *maki-e* design. Early nineteenth century. H. 1.5 in., L. 9 in.

READING STANDS—KENDAI, BONDAI

THE JAPANESE READING STAND—*kendai*—was originally used by imperial household members, the nobility, and priests to hold books and Buddhist scriptures. In later centuries it came to be a stand for music or literature used in the Japanese theater.

The earliest written language in Japan relied heavily on Chinese characters, terms, and concepts, since the writings had been brought from the mainland via Korea. In 405 A.D. a Korean was appointed tutor in Chinese to a Japanese imperial prince, and thus began a succession of classical language instructors from that country.

At the turn of the eighth century, two chronicles of Japanese history were compiled, one called the *Kojiki* (712) and the other the *Nihon Shoki* (720). These were the first Japanese historical and literary efforts with native insight that did not owe much to Chinese and Indian interpretations, although scholars agree that a great deal of the content is based on mythology rather than fact.

The first Japanese reading stand or *kendai* is reputed to be from this same Nara period (645–794) and kept in the Shosoin Imperial Treasure-house in Nara. The members of the imperial household, lords and their retainers, and select Buddhist and Shinto priests were the first to learn the art of reading and writing and thus would have had use for this furnishing.

Later, in the Muromachi period (1333–1573), use of the *kendai* extended into the world of the arts and entertainment, and it came to be used as an accessory in kabuki, bunraku, and dance performances. One of the most important musical instruments in Japan is the *shamisen*. Two major types of vocal music accompanied by the shamisen are the sung *nagauta* and the recitative *joruri* used in the puppet theater, bunraku. The singers or chanters would use highly decorated *kendai* on which to set their musical scores.

In more recent centuries, as literacy spread, the architecture of the Japanese house was modified to include a *shoin*, or reading room. This "study" or bay room originated with Zen Buddhism and then spread to the more wealthy class of educated landowners and scholars.

The *shoin* consists of a bay window covered with translucent paper in which a wide window shelf forms a reading desk. Under this is a cupboard for storage. Today the reading bay is no longer in use but is sometimes included purely as a decorative element.

Reading stands, usually in lustrous black lacquer decorated in gold *maki-e*, are found quite frequently in curio shops. They can always serve their original purpose for floor sitters, or if a lightweight *kendai* is discovered, it can make an ideal "in bed" reading stand. On a side table, a *kendai* is especially useful for holding the family dictionary or other heavy reference books.

Reading stand used in the Japanese puppet theater. Black lacquer on wood with gold *maki-e* and colored lacquer and mother-of-pearl inlay; red silk tassels hung from silver fittings. Late nineteenth century. H. 19 in.

SEALS—IN, HAN

THE JAPANESE SEAL or stamp, the *in* or *han*, owes its origin to China. It is known that by the beginning of the Shang dynasty (1500 B.C.) bronze seals were already in use, but their use was restricted for many centuries to royalty, the nobility, and high government officials. The early ones were worn as pendants around the neck.

In the ancient chronicles of Japan called the *Nihon Shoki* or *Nihongi* (part fact and part myth), the seal and its use is described and it is said to have arrived in Japan by 1 A.D. However, the earliest known seal in Japan is one beautifully carved in gold, which was excavated in 1784. According to its inscription, it was presented as a gift to the King of Na, an ancient Japanese kingdom in northern Kyushu, by the Chinese Han dynasty emperor, circa 57 A.D.

By the Nara period (710), seals had come into some popularity among the elite. The first mention of the official use of seals in Japan was about that same time. In an order issued by the Emperor Mombu in 704, he advised all provinces to make and use seals on all official documents.

It was not until the beginning of the Meiji period (circa 1870) that seals became commonly used, because until that time only people with social status were allowed last names. The common farmers, fishermen, merchants, and workmen had until that time used thumb marks as their legal signatures on contracts and notes of agreement.

Most seals are made of crystal, stone, wood, horn, ivory, or metal and are engraved with the family or personal name, or designs made up of several of the characters of the name or their parts. In some cases pictorial designs are used. They are carved in many sizes, from as small as the little finger to as large as five or six inches square. Old ones are often very difficult to read, even for scholars.

Many old *in* or *han* are beautifully carved, often in animal shapes, and when heavy enough they make wonderful paperweights or can be enjoyed as free-standing sculpture. It is also interesting to find old ones and have them recarved with your own name (or one you make up in Chinese characters) to use as stamps to identify books or as a seal for correspondence or art work. There are many antique seals available in Japan, and they still fall into a reasonable price category.

Pair of artist's seals. Chinese. Carved agate depicting mythical animals. Late eighteenth century. H. 4.5 in.

WRITING BOXES—SUZURI-BAKO

THE ART OF WRITING has always enjoyed a high regard in the East. Because of this, the Japanese writing or inkstone box, *suzuri-bako*, has long been among the most honored of objects. No time and effort were spared to make each one a unique work of lacquer art.

In the late Heian period (circa 900), Japanese art freed itself of outside influences, and a Japanese style of painting called *Yamato-e* was born. The most important representatives of this new style preserved in Japan today are the *Tales of Genji* hand scrolls, whose vivid illustrations show the refinements and intrigues of the court life of that period. Even utilitarian arts such as the lacquer craft, which previously had been devoted largely to objects of religious design and use, began to develop purely decorative themes based on the literature and poetry of the times. This new decorative style was to have a great influence on later Japanese art.

It is from the end of this era that the earliest extant example of the fitted Japanese inkstone box comes. A flat, oblong box with a lid that is sometimes slightly domed, it is sectioned to hold the inkstone (*suzuri*) for grinding the ink, the ink stick (*sumi*), a small metal water container (*mizuire*), and the writing brush (*fude*).

Many times the other objects used by the writer were made to match the *suzuri-bako*. The *ryoshi-bako* is a tall box, with one compartment, for holding paper. The *bundai* is a small writing table; the *shodana*, a bookcase with both open and closed compartments; and the *fubako* is a rectangular box, smaller than the writing box and tied with a colorful silken cord, used for transporting letters.

Writing boxes are usually decorated with some type of gold lacquer work. Many times a rather simple design on the top will be balanced by a surprising and delightfully intricate masterpiece on the inside of the lid, which, of course, can be seen only when the box is opened.

Writing boxes are still in use in modern Japan, and there are many antique *suzuri-bako* in the shops. Without the inside fittings, which are more often missing than not, they make beautiful accessories for holding stationery. However, because of the high value traditionally placed on the object itself and the fine craftsmanship that is usually evident in the lacquerwork, they are not inexpensive.

Writing box. Black lacquer on wood with pine tree design in gold *maki-e*. Late nineteenth century. 10.5 × 11.7 in.

Stationery box. Carved red lacquer on wood with flower and bird design. Nineteenth century. H. 3.5 in., L. 18.5 in.

BASKETS—KAGO

NEXT TO POTTERY, basketry has long been one of the most popular folkcrafts in Japan. Vessels are fashioned from bamboo, grass, bark, and vines into many useful shapes.

The mat and rope markings that characterize the pottery of the Jomon period indicate that this craft is roughly ten thousand years old.

Sen no Rikyu, the sixteenth century tea master, incorporated baskets into the tea ritual, especially for flowers, but also for holding charcoal for the fire and as tea caddies. Since that time bamboo flower vases and woven baskets for flowers have been favorites for use in this important ritual, especially in the spring, summer, and early autumn seasons.

The principles of ceremonial tea as taught by Rikyu incorporate harmony, reverence, purity, and calm with the avoidance of any ostentation or show of luxury. Simplicity and a "oneness with nature" are sought, and handcrafted objects are very much in tune with this philosophy. They are utilitarian and at the same time convey their own particular unrefined sense of beauty.

There are many wonderful bamboo baskets and containers still to be found in Japan today. Some are a warm, burnished brown, others lacquered in various colors, and still others retain their natural beige hue. They make aesthetically pleasing flower containers, since they bring the garden indoors and lend themselves well to natural arrangements. For a water container inside a basket, paint a can to match, or use a joint of bamboo. Bamboo is also lovely used separately for greenery. Baskets and bamboo are refreshing, natural companions to a small indoor rock garden.

Wide, flat-shaped baskets can be used for magazines and newspapers or dried flower arrangements, and still other shapes are ideal for foods such as fruit, or for salads if the basket is lacquered inside.

Woven vine or bamboo letter boxes date back many centuries. There is an example in the Shosoin Imperial Treasurehouse that was used to hold the calligraphic writings of the empress dowager in the seventh century. Both old and new ones can be seen today, and even in the twentieth century they make marvelous writing boxes.

Baskets. (L) Kyoto style, bamboo. Twentieth century. H. 14.5 in. (R) Braid style, woven bamboo. Twentieth century. H. 7 in.

STONE LANTERNS—ISHI-DORO

STONE LANTERNS, called *ishi-doro*, originated in Japan in temple and shrine services. In earliest times torches and bonfires were lit as part of the offering to the Shinto or Buddhist dieties. Fire was considered sacred and also effective in driving away demons and evil spirits. Soon, wooden and bronze lighted lanterns came to be used inside the temples and stone lanterns in the outer compounds.

The earliest stone lanterns known today were produced at the end of the seventh century in the Nara period (645–794). Many shapes of lanterns were designed at that time to complement the new Buddhist temple architecture.

Lighted lanterns gradually expanded from their primary religious function to include providing light for rooms or outdoor areas. Stone lanterns came to be used in the homes of the nobility as well as placed by roadsides to guide people at night.

From the Kamakura period (1185–1333) it became a popular custom for devotees and warriors to make gifts of stone or bronze lanterns to noted temples and shrines as prayers for good luck and fortune in personal life or in battle. The Kasuga Shrine in Nara is said to have nearly two thousand stone lanterns, some dating back to the eleventh century. These lanterns are usually the same style. Thus any lantern of this shape is called *kasuga*.

The tea masters are credited with bringing the stone lantern into the garden, where they were useful in guiding the guests at dawn and evening tea. They were later used more to add charm and interest to the setting than for illumination. Specific rules were made regarding their placement in the garden in order to be in harmony with the trees and rocks.

Most stone lantern shapes are named either after the Buddhist temples where they were conceived or refer to the tea master whose design they were, such as Rikyu and Oribe.

Stone lanterns can be found in limitless styles and sizes and remain a beautiful, serene focal point in either an indoor or outdoor garden.

Lantern. Stone. Early nineteenth century. H. approx. 6 ft.

TEA KETTLES—CHA-GAMA

TEA KETTLES, *cha-gama*, made especially for the ceremony of tea drinking, were first seen at the end of the Muromachi period (1333–1573). There had been iron kettles for cooking purposes much earlier, but when the tea drinking rites became popular, the kettles came to be treated as art objects.

The ritual of drinking tea, called *cha-no-yu* or *chado*, teaches a viewpoint toward life that has influenced virtually the entire society of Japan, as well as its arts, for more than four hundred years. It combines aesthetics and etiquette, and embraces all classes of people. Once inside the tea room, all class distinctions are dropped.

In the beginning, the tea cult was closely tied to Zen Buddhism imported from China. It was practiced in Zen monasteries during the early Kamakura period (circa 1200). One hundred years later, tea drinking had spread among the nobility and military classes and eventually it developed into a kind of ritual for entertaining guests. At the same time, a new school was established in Nara that introduced the ideas of quiet and peace as being the essence of the tea cult. In the Momoyama period (1573–1614), Sen no Rikyu incorporated these ideas into the tea ceremony that is still practiced today in Japan.

The village of Ashiya on the island of Kyushu became famous for their kettles, called *Ashiya-gama*. They are characterized by a smooth surface with elegant design work. *Temmyo-gama*, produced in another region, were also much in demand and possessed an unpretentious quality in their rough, plain surfaces. These kettles or urns were cast in metal in round shapes, with no spout, since the water for tea was taken from them with a bamboo dipper.

All this attention focused on the ceremonial tea implements also affected the serving of ordinary green tea, and beautiful pots were made in pottery, porcelain, and later, pewter.

Today there are a variety of beautifully crafted antique kettles and teapots that fall within a price range available to all. The *cha-gama* is a kettle or urn, *tetsubin* an iron kettle, *chabin* and *dobin* teapots. The iron kettles produce an extraordinary cup of tea, since they seem to bring out the more subtle flavors of the Japanese and Chinese teas. Additionally, teapots or kettles are lovely filled with fresh flowers or greenery.

Tea kettle. Etched copper. Late nineteenth century. H. 7.5 in.

BROCADES—NISHIKI

SILK BROCADE, *nishiki*, was one of the first luxuries imported into Japan from China. Shortly thereafter the Japanese began to produce their own brocades for use by the imperial family and court nobles.

The art of weaving as such is believed to have begun in Japan in the period of the Yayoi culture (200 B.C.–200 A.D.). The earliest written records describe sewing women being sent by the king of Paekche to the Japanese court around 300 A.D. Paekche was one of the Three Kingdoms of ancient Korea. Even at this time Korea was acting as an intermediary for Chinese culture flowing into Japan.

During the Asuka and Nara periods (552–794), there was a great influx of Chinese culture of the brilliant T'ang dynasty, which accompanied the spread of Buddhism in Japan. The textile craft, along with others, progressed tremendously at this time, and during Empress Suiko's reign the following was recorded at a ceremonial event: "At this time the Imperial Princes, the Princess, and the Court Nobles all wore gold headdresses and used garments made of brocade with purple embroidery of varicolored, figured silk, or of silk gauze."

The progress of the industry was not remarkable during the ensuing Heian, Kamakura, and Muromachi periods. However, with the development of the tea cult in the latter half of the fifteenth century, a strong new emphasis was put on exotic imported fabrics. The "celebrated fabrics," as they were called, were used for tea caddies, made into pouches to hold tea implements, and as mountings for paintings and calligraphy hung at the tea ceremony ritual. This emphasis on elaborate textiles caused Japanese craftsmen to imitate and improve upon these imported designs, and a great revival of the industry took place during the following Momoyama period (1573–1614).

Dutch fabrics also were imported about this same time, giving further stimulation to the growing textile trade.

An important factor was the lady's kimono. It had become simplified through the centuries, and the innermost layer during Heian times, had come to be used by itself as an outer garment. This called for much larger and more elaborate pictorial designs to be woven into this new outer kimono.

The institution of the Noh drama in Muromachi times and kabuki performances in the early Edo period (1614–1868), along with the other arts, gave a great impetus to the weaving of artistic brocades, and in the middle Edo period the textile art reached a new high.

Old Japanese Noh and kabuki costumes and *obis* (the cummerbund and back tie of the Japanese kimono) are often made of opulent brocades whose patterns are too intricate and costly to be produced today. Unique examples of the heights reached in Japanese textiles, they make stunning wall panels, cushion covers, and have many other interior design uses. They are also lovely made into evening suits and wraps.

Cushions. Silk brocade (*obi*). Early twentieth century. 12 × 12 in., 12 × 20 in.

KIMONOS

THE JAPANESE WORD *kimono* means clothing. Although no examples of very ancient Japanese textile art have survived, *haniwa* clay figures of the Tumulus period (200–552) show that the mode of dress, even then, was decorative, most outer garments having designs or patterns in the cloth. The main garment for women seems to have been a coat and skirt called *kinumo* ("silk cloth").

The early stimulus for Japanese textiles and clothing came from China via Korea. During the Asuka and Nara periods (552–794) the official dress was of Chinese style, and wearing apparel was made of figured brocade silk or silk gauze. Braided sashes and embroidered footwear were also worn.

In following Heian times (794–1185) textiles as well as the products of other crafts became "Japanized." The common people of this day wore a simple kimono with relatively short and narrow sleeves as their everyday costume, but court ladies' attire, sometimes referred to as the "twelve-layer dress," consisted of layers of undergarments of various colors and a long pleated skirt tied around the waist over the outer robe and spreading out broadly in back.

The Kamakura era (1185–1333) brought simplification to this court costume, and various layers were eliminated until finally the *kosode*, which had been the innermost layer, came to the surface. In the latter part of this period there appeared a form called "*kosode* and *hakama*," in which loose culotte type trousers, *hakama*, were worn over the tucked-in *kosode*. Later in the Muromachi period (1333–1573), this was further simplified by elimination of the *hakama*, and the usual women's dress became the *kosode* alone. *Hakama* continued to be worn by men, however.

In subsequent years, the *kosode* changed from its image of inner apparel into a garment in which large, elaborate, pictorial designs were used. This is what we now know as the modern kimono.

Old kimonos make elegant and uniquely beautiful lounging or hostess robes. Since they are intended to be folded over at the waist, there is usually enough extra material with which to make a matching belt or cummerbund. Each one is an original, with a breathtaking profusion of hand-dyed patterns, many of which are too expensive to be duplicated today. *Hakama*, worn by Japanese male and female dancers, actors, and musicians, can also make attractive evening pants when stitched up at the sides. They are usually in soft taffetas or metallic brocades and are lovely worn over a black evening sheath or sweater.

Kimono sleeve. Iris pattern dyed and embroidered on silk. Early twentieth century.

CRESTS—MON

FOR HUNDREDS OF YEARS the elegant chrysanthemum has been the royal emblem of Japan. It was an auspicious flower brought to Japan from China. Reputed to be both sacred and representative of a long life, it gained great popularity as a motif for clothing and table utensils.

The twelfth century Emperor Gotoba loved this flower and is said to have been the first who used it on his swords, vehicles, and clothes.

In those colorful days of the Heian court, the movement of the nobles was easy to check (gossip was a favorite pastime) as they ostentatiously marked all their possessions, including their richly lacquered oxcarts, with their family symbol, or *mon*.

It was at the end of the following Kamakura Period (1185–1333) that the crest, or *monsho*, of the sixteen-petal chrysanthemum came to be reserved for the exclusive use of the emperor. The paulownia leaf became the crest of the empress.

Crests were important insignias of family unity and were representative of the position, taste, and honor of the family. The motifs selected were often from nature and given great consideration before they were officially adopted. These early examples of Japanese graphic art were elegant and simple. They remain fresh and vital even today.

The Kamakura military families had needs different from those of the aristocracy. They designed crests that were bold, legible designs easily recognizable on the battlefield. Around bright banners decorated with these clan symbols they could quickly mobilize their men.

In the peaceful Edo Period (1614–1868) crests were used to clarify rank in the new, rigid feudal system. By identification of the mon, its bearer could be given the level of treatment to which he was entitled.

At this same time, newly rich merchant families began to adopt the use of crests to boast of their recently acquired power. Their choice of design was much more flamboyant than that of the old aristocracy, and their crests were known as *date-mon*, or dandyish crests.

Merchants also began to create symbols for their businesses, and these were dyed into curtains and the employees' work clothes and carved on signboards advertising the shops. Many of these are still in use today.

Crests are often found on old kimonos and household utensils such as porcelain dishes and lacquer boxes, tables, and trays.

Plate. Blue–and–white porcelain picturing the imperial chrysanthemum crest with sixteen petals. Early nineteenth century. D. 14 in.

DOLLS—NINGYO

DOLLS, OR NINGYO, were used as talismans and charms in ancient Japan, as in other primitive civilizations. The earliest records from the Heian period (794–1185) show that dolls made of paper or grass were used on annual festival days to guard against illness and other misfortunes. Also, dolls called *hina* in the shape of little girls and boys were fashioned and used as playthings for the children of the nobility. They were often taught to make these dolls themselves.

From the Asian continent came the art of puppetry, and in Japan strolling showmen traveled throughout the country begging for alms as they operated their figures. Buddhist priests, too, often used puppets and dolls to illustrate their stories while preaching. It was a time of highly elaborate manners and customs, and dolls came to take a prominent place in the social occasions of the people.

It was not until the much later Edo period (1614–1868) that doll-making made a definite advance, and many and varied dolls came to be looked upon as works of art.

Some of the representative types of Japanese dolls from that era include colored wooden dolls in the likeness of nude babies, which were used as playtoys, and dolls that portrayed people in various walks of life. The latter were carved in wood and painted colorfully on those parts representing clothing.

Others were dolls in clothes, such as wooden dolls with clothing pasted on; genre dolls that represented the people of different social classes; naked dolls that could be clothed at home; and a doll movable at the joints, which was often a "portrait doll" after a favorite child or famous personality of the day.

Special dolls for children's festivals became popular for display on Girls' Day in March and Boys' Day celebrated in May. Primitive wooden *kokeshi* dolls were originally children's playtoys in northern Japan but became souvenirs to be collected on trips. Clay and papier-mâché dolls were made in the rural areas and used as toys, since they were low in price. Hakata (now Fukuoka City) and Fushimi became the centers of clay doll production.

Also in the Edo period the shogun's gifts to his retainers were given in *obunkyo-ningyo*, which are "receptacle dolls" of papier-mâché that depict samurai, court ladies, animals, and characters from Japanese mythology. They can still be found today, but many have the bottom half missing.

It became fashionable to place china or bronze dolls in the *tokonoma*, "picture alcove," of the home, either replacing or alongside the flower arrangement.

Elaborately costumed dolls sold frequently today in department stores usually represent young maidens performing well-known Japanese dances.

Doll-making is taught in special schools throughout Japan, and dolls continue to play an active part in the customs of the people.

Doll. Gesso on wood; movable joints. Late eighteenth century. H. 8 in.

INK LINE—SUMI-TSUBO

THE JAPANESE SUMI-TSUBO, used to draw straight lines, has been in use by carpenters, masons, and other construction workers for many centuries and is still used today. It is made of wood with one end containing a spool to hold a long length of strong string and the other end hollowed out into a shallow bowl to hold cotton saturated with *sumi*, or black ink. The string or cord is pulled through the ink, drawn taut, and then lifted near the center and quickly released to snap back into place and produce a straight line.

An interesting story accompanies the earliest written reference to the *sumi-tsubo* in the *Nihongi*, the ancient Chronicles of Japan. In around 469 A.D., the current emperor was fascinated with the great dexterity of one of his carpenters called Mane and asked if he ever occasioned to make a mistake. The confident master carpenter replied, "I never make a mistake!" which the emperor silently decided to take as a challenge.

He called forth the palace ladies-in-waiting and ordered them to strip off their clothes, leaving only their waist-cloths, and wrestle with one another. Mane, fascinated with the scene, could not help but stop and watch for awhile, but presently he returned to his work. Inadvertently, he soon made a slight mistake. The emperor immediately rebuked him for having spoken so hastily of his ability for perfection and ordered him executed on the moor.

A friend and comrade in his lament for Mane composed the following poem:

> The much to be regretted
> Carpenter of Winabe —
> The ink cord he applied, —
> When he is no more,
> Who will apply it?
> Alas! that ink-cord!

The lament came to the ears of the emperor who, regretting his harsh decision, sent a messenger by fast horse to pardon the carpenter. His life thus spared, the carpenter in turn composed an ode to the swift black horse of Kahi, whose speed had saved him.

A miniature relative of the *sumi-tsubo* was once used in dressmaking, and an example from the seventh century is preserved in the imperial treasurehouse. Instead of ink, white powder was used to mark lines on cloth. Since all the lines in the kimono are straight, it was a most effective tool.

Ink line. Wood and string. Late nineteenth century. L. 11.5 in., H. 5 in.

MAP PLATES

MAP PLATES, in blue-and-white porcelain, were made late in the Edo period (1614–1868) when the Tokugawa rulers had successfully unified Japan and closed it to outside commerce.

To keep the landowning gentry in line, it was required that they spend one year in Edo (Tokyo) and one year in their home province, alternately. This forced the overlords to maintain large establishments in both places and take at least one major trip a year. The system effectively used much of their time, energy, and finances and served its intended purpose of keeping the country at peace.

It also served to create a busy network of inner communications. In fact, by 1633, there was a regular messenger service offering three classes of delivery. The usual was a thrice-monthly service between Edo and Kyoto and Osaka, taking ten to twelve days. A slower service took up to twenty-five days, and a superexpress (available only to officials) took just a little over three days. Considering the messengers ran on foot in relays all the way, our modern postal system does not seem to have progressed much!

These local rulers, called daimyo, and their retainers, the samurai, naturally developed a healthy interest in the geography of Japan as they traveled back and forth and kept tabs on their neighbors.

This same era saw the rise of the merchant class, with the new peace bringing prosperity and a great trading boom within the country. Originally at the bottom of the class system, the merchant class rose to influence as Japan changed from a feudal to a commercial society. The merchants were highly competitive and always looked for new or faster trade routes, and so they too exhibited a newfound interest in the terrain of the country.

These two groups became ideal customers for the new map plates that came to be made. In addition to these unique and beautiful porcelain maps, used mainly as status symbols for display, hand-drawn and woodblock printed maps, *chizu*, came into popularity.

Sometimes charts were a part of the maps, giving distances in *ri* from the major cities and provinces in relation to the capitol at Edo. One *ri* is approximately 2.5 miles.

Map plates. Blue-and-white porcelain. Late nineteenth century. Round, D. 15 in., square, 11 × 8 in.

MEDICINE CHESTS—KUSURI-DANSU

MEDICINE CHESTS, *kusuri-dansu*, are small, wooden chests with multiple tiny drawers for holding various medicines.

These interesting chests, as in the case of Japanese medicine, were originally imported from Korea.

The earliest mention of medicine is in the *Nihon Shoki*, the early Chronicles of Japan. Emperor Ingio (412 A.D.) had become crippled after reaching manhood and could not walk. After some years, a physician was called from the Korean kingdom of Silla to attend the emperor, and shortly thereafter he was cured.

It is believed that the ancient treatment of acupuncture, recently winning renewed popularity, was introduced to Japan from China in the sixth century.

In the early seventh century, during the reign of Empress Suiko, a Korean physician schooled in Chinese medicine arrived in Japan from the Korean kingdom of Paekche, bringing with him many medicinal herbs. These became the foundation of Japanese medicine until the introduction of Dutch medicine in the sixteenth century. This was discarded in favor of German medicinal practices in the nineteenth century.

Even after the introduction of Western medicine, the use of herb medicine remained popular and is still practiced in Japan today. Called *furidashi*, it consists of boiling herbs, roots, and barks in water and taking the liquid to cure various ills. Korean ginseng, largely touted today as an aphrodisiac, is one of the most famous medicines of this type. While it was once considered a miracle cure, modern medicine limits its restorative powers to relieving fatigue, stimulating the metabolism, and improving digestion.

Kuroyaki is a type of Japanese medicine introduced at the end of the eighteenth century. It is a powder of charred plants and animals purported to give vitality and cure diseases.

In addition to traditional medicines, a great many home cures were popular. Most involve roots and plants not readily available, but here are two that might be easy to try. To cure a hangover, boil cloves and drink the water while hot. To soften rough skin, put saké in the bathwater.

Chests used by shops selling medicinal herbs come in all sizes and shapes. Many times the tiny drawers have individual brass pulls, and the names of the medicines are written on the front of each drawer. They make great sewing or utility cabinets and are ideal for storing collections of small objects such as *netsuke*, *inro*, jade, and snuff bottles.

Medicine chest. Red lacquer on wood with iron fittings. Late nineteenth century, modern finish. H. 29.5 in.

METAL DOOR PULLS—HIKITE

THE HIKITE OR METAL DOOR PULL of the Japanese sliding door is an example of the fineness and versatility of Japanese metalwork.

In the traditional Japanese structure, one sits on the floor, and the act itself is not purely for physical comfort as it is in the West, but is at once spiritual, physical, and mental. Man becomes an island surrounded by space.

The purpose of Japanese architecture was to coordinate this space with the natural setting. Great thought was given to every finishing detail that would lend itself to this concept. The *hikite* was at eye level when seated, therefore beauty in addition to utility was important.

The earliest metalwork in Japan, from the prehistoric period, included bronze and iron swords, armor, bells, and mirrors.

In the Asuka period (552–645), Buddhism promoted a strong advance in metalwork. There was great demand for Buddhist sculpture and various implements used in the ritual of this new religion.

The next upsurge was in the twelfth century, when the military dictators required large quantities of weapons and armor, and later a new influence, the tea ceremony, was felt. This required decoration of kettles and other tea ceremony equipment.

In the era of great castles and mansions, the sixteenth and seventeenth centuries, a new demand for metalwork was created in architectural fittings. One of these was the ornamental door pull.

The earliest form was a recessed metal plate through which two short cords of silk were tied in a special knot with tassels. This cord was the handle by which the door was moved back and forth. The cord eventually disappeared and the metal plate came to be elaborately decorated.

Flowers and animals were popular natural themes, as were designs inspired by artistic pursuits such as Noh masks and writing brushes. Many *hikite* were designed to harmonize with the paintings on the sliding doors for which they were being made.

The ornamental door pull is one of the few antiques still available today at reasonable prices. On many the metal craftsmanship is so superb they lend themselves to display on small stands, while the more common variety could be used as individual nut dishes or ashtrays.

Door pulls. Embossed, plated, engraved, and lacquered metal. Late nineteenth century. Average D. 3 in.

MONEY BOXES, CHESTS—ZENI-BAKO, ZENI-DANSU

MONEY BOXES, *zeni-bako*, and money chests, *zeni-dansu*, came into wide use among the merchant class during the Edo era (1614–1868). They were used to contain coins, to transport and store large sums of money, and to protect their contents from burglary. They could not be easily broken and could bear great weights, since they were made of hard woods such as *keyaki*, cypress, or oak and reinforced with metal hardware.

Their strength and robust quality, especially in the design of the metalwork, gives them a certain aesthetic appeal even though they were designed principally for utilitarian purposes.

Various styles were used, one with a flat upper lid and a slot for the coins, some with a funnel-shaped upper lid and coin slot, and others in a simple coffin style. Many were constructed with hidden inner drawers.

The first copper coin was minted in Japan in 708 but did not come into popular use at that time. In the fourteenth century a limited amount of Chinese, Korean, and Annamese coins were imported and circulated. However, until the early 1600s, general trade among Japanese society was done by barter.

Japan's first coin to enjoy general popularity was the *zeni*, a copper coin minted in 1636 (hence the name *zeni-bako*). Gold and silver coins followed soon after. While copper coins were in use throughout the country, in addition gold was the Edo currency, and Osaka and Kyoto used silver. This created a somewhat erratic monetary exchange involving considerable transshipping of funds and created a steady demand for coin containers.

At this same time some merchants in need of small change began to write out the various amounts owed on slips of paper, and the feudal lords issued their own clan notes. Thus a certain type of "paper money" came into use even though it was prohibited by the central government.

In the early Meiji era (1868–1912) the government issued paper money, and modern banks were established that issued their own notes. This flooded the country with an assortment of paper money. In 1901 the currency was standardized, and only the Bank of Japan remained authorized to issue paper money.

Some money boxes have their commercial firm name branded into the wood in several places. This method of identifying personal property was popular with the merchants and country people. The daimyo and wealthy gentry used the *mon*, or family crest, as a monogram with which to decorate objects and denote ownership.

The rustic strength and simple beauty of old money boxes make them a joy to own and use.

Money and personal accessories box. *Keyaki* wood and iron. Nineteenth century. H. 10 in.

Cash box. Wood and iron. Merchant's name "Tomiya" branded on wood. Late nineteenth century. H. 9 in., L. 15 in.

NAILHEAD COVERS—KUGIKAKUSHI

KUGIKAKUSHI, DECORATIVE NAILHEAD COVERS, came into widespread use in the sixteenth and seventeenth centuries. They provided a decorative metal covering for the joints of the huge beams and posts of shrines and temples and also the great castles and mansions that were constructed for various feudal lords.

Japanese metalwork was a sophisticated and complex craft, and many new alloys and techniques were achieved that remain unique to Japan. The metal artist was highly esteemed and had his own set of tools that often numbered more than two hundred pieces. When swords were banned in 1871 by government edict, many craftsmen were forced into new outlets, and so the minor metal arts flourished.

Nailhead covers were usually cast in metal from molds or occasionally hand-wrought, and the surface was then finished in varying techniques. Some of the decorative methods include engraving the design on the mold, which creates an embossed pattern on the metal; openwork; chiseling or engraving on the finished object; inlay with small strips of gold, silver, or other metals tapped into grooves; fusion of gold and silver foil to the surface; plating; lacquering and enameling.

So many metal alloys were used that it is difficult to determine the base metal of most objects. *Shakudo* containes copper and gold, and a glossy patina of dark brown or bluish black is obtained. *Shibuichi* is silver and copper and produces dark gray tones. White metal, or *shirogane*, came from lead ore with silver, and there are many other combinations. Decorative motifs for many centuries played a prominent role in both the religious and daily lives of the Japanese people. Architecture was embellished with these symbols, which were representative of both the tangibles of nature and the intangibles of the spirit. Cranes, sparrows, bats, turtles, bamboo, and family crests, were some of the popular subjects for nailhead covers.

These unusual works of art are interesting and lovely examples of early Japanese metalwork. Search for a matching pair for drawer pulls, give one as a gift for a paperweight, or use a group of them on a decorative panel. They are sure to be conversation pieces.

Nailhead covers. Embossed, cast, plated, enameled, pierced, and etched metal. Nineteenth, early twentieth centuries. Average D. 3 in.

SHOP SIGNS—KANBAN

IN THE EARLY DAYS of Japan, as villages sprouted, there arose a communal need for goods and services. As shops were established to fill these needs, most often being an extension of the home, the earliest foundations of advertising were laid in the use of a sign to designate the shop and its product.

Shop signs, *kanban*, had two functions. The first was to announce the business of the shop in a catchy and appealing manner, and the second to take the ravages of inclement weather throughout many years. Thick, sturdy planks of wood were used, often sculpted into the shape of the product being sold. The name of the product or service was deeply incised to make it weatherproof.

The wig maker, catering to the roving theatrical troupes, had a sign in the shape of a head with the natural wood representing the shaved pate and the side locks and topknot painted in black lacquer. The tea ceremony utensil store was represented by a large round hibachi with a kettle sitting on top. The stone cutter featured a sign in the shape of a stone lantern, while the *bangasa* shop had a closed umbrella as its trademark. Seal makers branded their signs with various samples, and mirror craftsmen sometimes inlaid a sample of their product into their signs. The early signs were simple and naive. Later signs became more refined, and trade names, crests, and family names were used.

It was during the Edo period (1614–1868) that the merchant class rose to prominence and power, and firm names and insignia came to be recognized as reliable symbols of the house or shop and its products.

The merchants invented their own crests, called *date-mon*, or dandyish crests, imitating the aristocracy. Often the company insignia was made up of the first character of the founder's name enclosed in a circle, square, or diamond. This symbol was carved on the wooden signboard hung outside the shop and dyed on the *noren*, curtains hung over the entrance to keep out the street dust and flies. It was also dyed into the center back of the servants' or employees' clothing or uniform. This custom is still practiced today in many places, especially in saké shops, among construction workers, and in countryside businesses. Tourists know these loose fitting jackets as "happy coats."

Shop sign. Color on wood. The merchandise pictured includes a pipe, comb, and writing materials. Nineteenth century. 35.5 × 21 in.

CHESTS—OT-CHANG

KOREAN CHESTS have a long and illustrious history and have always been considered one of that country's specialties in craftsmanship.

The tombs of the Han dynasty's Lo-lang colony (ca. 30 B.C.) have rendered many spectacular artifacts. Included are weapons and chariots, religious objects such as bronze mirrors, and household goods, among which are chests (Japanese: *tansu*; Korean: *ot-chang*).

During the long Yi dynasty (1392–1910), the basic types of household furnishings remained unchanged and consisted mainly of carved, lacquered, or inlaid storage chests, tables, and folding screens.

Korean furniture is classic in its simple, clean, and beautiful lines. The wood craftsmen made good use of every kind of wood that was obtainable locally, such as pine, ginko, pagoda tree, paulownia, pear, and persimmon, often using them in interesting combinations.

The hardware found on Korean furniture also has a quiet distinction of its own. Iron is common and is assertive yet elegant; yellow and white brass are used on the more luxurious pieces; occasionally silver is also found.

Korean chests available today may be classified into two general categories: the large bin-shaped storage containers of the farmers, and the more elaborate chests of the aristocracy.

The former were sturdy utility boxes, used for everything from rice to bedding, and were reinforced with simple, bold metalwork.

For the more prosperous, chests ranged in size from ceiling-high wardrobes to tiny, carved, lacquered, or inlaid accessory boxes. The tall wardrobes, sometimes in two or more sections, feature a hollow box construction with wooden doors opening outward. Often there is a small half-shelf inside. Floral and butterfly motifs are common on the metal fittings.

Another type, resembling a desk or side table, has drawers and refined metal fittings. These chests often have gracefully curved legs and scroll-shaped tops.

Old medicine chests have a myriad of tiny drawers. The names of the medicines are often painted or carved on the front of the drawer,

The beautiful locks that often accompany Korean chests are collectors' items in their own right.

Chest. Mixture of woods with iron fittings. Late nineteenth century. H. 37 in.

METALWORK

A CERTAIN DELICACY and refined beauty has always pervaded the metalwork of Korea. The earliest pieces of this art that are extant today are from the Transition Period (3rd–1st century B.C.). They include horse bits, mirrors, belt hooks, and relics whose purpose is still undetermined.

From the Lo-lang period tombs (1st–3rd century A.D.), are found such objects as a tongued buckle inlaid with gold and precious stones and a beautifully engraved metal scroll holder with flying figures of animals and huntsmen against an imaginative background of mountains, trees, and cloud forms. In much of the early Korean metalwork and bronzes from both these periods, the origins are obviously not Chinese. It is believed that the influences came directly from the ancient Middle Eastern Scythian art of the steppes in southern Russia via Siberia.

Further influences from the Eurasian steppes can be found in the unique golden crowns and accessories of the Old Silla dynasty of the sixth century. The crowns bear the early religious symbols of this nomadic culture—the tree and deer antlers. It has also been theorized that the elaborate gold belts and ornamental buckles of this same period are more closely related to barbarian girdles of the nomadic tribes than to the Chinese. It is possible that Turkish silverwork was also known in Korea, entering either by way of the Chinese mainland or perhaps directly from the Middle East by ship.

Whatever its ancient origins, it is clear that from the beginning the Koreans took the craft of casting and working gold, silver, bronze, and other metals and developed it into an art form uniquely their own.

Even today their expertise can be seen in the metal fittings on both antique and new Korean chests. Often the work is cutout, etched, and delicate, while at other times it is extremely bold and monumental. Either style easily denotes its Korean origin.

Box. Black lacquer on wood with mother-of-pearl inlay, brass fittings. Late Yi dynasty, nineteenth century. 10 × 4.75 × 4.75 in.

Metal box. Iron inlaid with silver. Yi dynasty, eighteenth century. 2.4 × 4.25 × 3 in.

PAINTED OXHORN—HWAGAK

HWAGAK, OR PAINTED OXHORN, is one of the most interesting and colorful of the Korean minor arts. From the time of Christ, the Korean arts of lacquer, metalwork, and woodwork have enjoyed a spirit of simplicity and a sense of refinement that are peculiar to their local culture, even though much of the art impetus was imported.

Korean wood and bamboo work is a highly regarded art form that is of early origin and has a unique essence. In the Yi dynasty (1392–1910), and possibly earlier, a new style of decorating wooden boxes appeared, called *hwagak*. This is woodwork faced with pieces of painted oxhorn.

The oxhorn is converted into thin sheets of various sizes and shapes; then scenes, such as birds and flowers, animals, and figures, are painted in bright primary colors on the underside. Next, the horn is glued to a wooden box frame, and thin strips of white are inlaid between the sheets of colored horn to form geometric patterns and bond the pieces together. Delicately wrought metal fasteners and corner braces (often in tiny flower shapes) are added for both sturdiness and beauty. The result is a stained-glass effect. Since the paint is on the underside, the strong colors shining through do not easily fade or rub off, but remain bright and clear.

Finely etched locks complete the metalwork. The insides of the boxes are either finished in lacquer, lined in handmade paper, or the two methods are combined.

In recent years a few imitations have appeared on the market, so it is wise to be cautious. In the imitations the painting is on plastic rather than oxhorn.

The boxes (in square, rectangular, round, hexagonal, and casket shapes) were used for the luxuries of aristocrats and also by the common people for small treasures and accessories.

As with many other of the Korean folk arts and handcrafts, a simple, naive beauty radiates from these brightly colored oxhorn boxes.

Boxes for personal accessories. Painted oxhorn on wood with metal fittings. Nineteenth century. H. 5 in.

SCHOLAR'S STUDY PAINTINGS—CHAEKKORI

KOREAN PAINTINGS showing a stylized portrayal of the accessories of a scholar's study are known as *chaekkori*. *Chaek* means books, and *kori*, a scene in a puppet play.

These Korean still life paintings have a realism coupled with a charming naivety in their picturization of this favorite topic related to cultural and academic pursuits. Most *chaekkori* are done by unknown folk artists and unsigned, but they are an important contribution to the native arts of Korea. They represent a favorite Chinese subject that has been made purely and distinctively Korean in its final form. While the Korean artists of the academy and nobility were doing work based on Chinese techniques, the artists of the people were painting the creatures of nature. Subjects such as birds, tigers, fish and other topics based on folk stories are filled with good humor, satire, and animation.

Scholar's study paintings usually depict stacks of books along with the scholar's four friends—the inkstone, ink stick, brush, and paper. Besides these, there was a wealth of other articles for the artist to choose from. There were desks, bookshelves, and stationery chests; for taking care of brushes there were brush holders, racks, caps, and washers; there were paperweights, inkstone stands, and water droppers. Depending on the scholar's social status and pocketbook, there might be luxuries such as flower vases, hanging scrolls, and calligraphy.

Chaekkori were usually painted in sets of six or eight panels mounted on separate hanging scrolls. Each picture, in addition to the scholar's objects, might feature a flower or fruit of the different seasons. Symbolic foods such as pomegranates, grapes, and tangerines, all representative of fertility and wealth, were favorites.

One popular object seen in almost every set of scholar's study paintings are Western eyeglasses, probably introduced by the Jesuits in the early eighteenth century.

Scholar's study painting. Colors on paper. Yi dynasty, nineteenth century. 22 × 12 in.

SCREENS—PYONGP'UNG

ANTIQUE KOREAN SCREENS, *pyongp'ung*, can trace their ancestry back at least as far as the first century A.D. and were probably in use long before that.

The ancient Han Chinese Lo-lang colony was located a few miles outside of P'yongyang in what is now North Korea. To this major trading outpost the Chinese brought their own culture and set up workshops in which Chinese artisans and their Korean helpers worked side by side. Thus, the tastes and abilities of the two peoples were slowly blended to form what would be the foundations of all subsequent Korean art.

The tombs of this colony, excavated early in this century by the Japanese, brought forth a great wealth of artifacts, among them, standing screens.

In the fourteenth century Korea introduced a new type of screen, which revolutionized screen painting and composition. Until this time, a folding screen consisted of a group of separate wooden panels with brocaded borders, tied together by means of cords passing through holes pierced at the vertical edges of the panels. In the new Korean innovation, the leaves were joined by paper hinges built into the body of the screen before the silk or paper for painting was pasted on. A brocade border extended over the composite whole. In the former style, the continuity of design was broken by the frame and brocade. In the new style the tightly joined leaves offered either one surface for painting a picture or greater unity among separate picture panels.

In eighteenth century China, during the Ch'ing reign, art began catering to middle-class tastes. The same trend became apparent during the concurrent Edo period in Japan, where a new merchant class arose. However, in Korea there existed no middle class. Art was the prerogative of the cultured elite, the members of the court. The products were painstakingly turned out in limited quantity, with the majority of high artistic merit. In this Korean art, which owed most of its impetus and techniques to China, there was a lack of the slick refinement attained by its neighbors at this same period. Instead there was a simple, naive quality that|today makes Korean art distinctive.

Folding screens of the Yi dynasty (1392–1910) are usually painted or embroidered. Subjects include palace scenes, hunting scenes, and genre scenes picturing rural communities. There are also many bird and flower paintings and landscapes; animals, especially in pairs—denoting connubial bliss—are another popular subject.

The Korean screens available today fall mainly into a folk art category. Their wit, charm, and distinctive naivete make them highly appealing.

Hunting screen panel Colors on paper. Yi dynasty, eighteenth century. H. 43.5 in.

SILLA DYNASTY POTTERY

THE SPONTANEITY, individuality, and sturdy simplicity of Korean Silla dynasty ceramics makes them highly attractive to our generation raised on mass-produced, mold-made objects. In recent years many of the old tombs at the ancient capitol of Kyongju have been excavated and many others robbed of their contents, bringing a flood of Silla relics into the antique market.

The Three Kingdoms period in Korea (circa 57 B.C.–668 A.D.) was a time when the country was divided into three parts, the Koguryo dynasty in the north, the Paekche dynasty in the central eastern section, and the Old Silla dynasty in the southwest. In 668 the Silla (pronounced Shilla) rulers defeated their neighbors and gained control of the entire peninsula, resulting in the United Silla kingdom (668–935), with its capitol at Kyongju.

Korean Silla pottery came into its full development during the fifth and sixth centuries. While there is an undeniable Chinese influence due to the immigration of people prior to this time and to the fact that many shapes owe their origin to Chinese bronze and clay forms of an earlier date, the interpretation and freedom of expression in Silla pottery is uniquely Korean. Their natural, free quality and their sturdy architectural feeling make them ever appealing and fresh.

The majority of Silla pots are stoneware and fired at a high enough temperature to produce a clear ring when struck. The color is usually dark gray to black, and there are sometimes stamped or incised patterns. Covered stem cups for food storage, drinking cups, large storage jars, varishaped bottles, and oil lamps are a few of the pottery shapes that have been excavated.

Silla ceramics are basically utilitarian and functional, but earlier Silla pieces are often dignified by a stand ranging from a few inches in height to more than a foot. These stands usually have stylized perforations, an important decorative motif of this era.

Silla dynasty ceramics are sometimes found in Japan and abound in Korea. They can be taken out of the country only with the proper export permission ascertaining they are not considered cultural properties. Kilns in the Kyongju area are also now producing excellent copies, but beware that the prices of such are not for original pieces.

Stemmed food vessel. Stoneware with molded and openwork designs. United Silla kingdom, ninth century. H. 9 in.

KORYO CELADONS

KOREAN CERAMICS were held in little regard other than as an offshoot of the Chinese, until around 1880. At that time the graves of the Koryo dynasty (918–1392) began to be opened, and astounding treasures came forth.

So beautiful were the burial accessories—delicately incised and molded bowls; slender, beautifully curved pitchers inlaid in black and white; refined, lotus-shaped pots, all in shades varying from ivory white to soft, deep celadon blue greens—that the world viewpoint changed overnight. Not only were the Koryo celadons acclaimed as the most brilliant art form in Korean history, but some experts called them the finest ceramics ever produced in the world.

A noted scholar-writer of the concurrent Sung dynasty in China (960–1279) sang the praises of the wonderful Koryo celadon thusly: "The Academy (Peking) has the finest books and our palaces harbor the choicest wines, Canton has the best in inkstones, Anhui excels in ink and Fukien in tea; but the secret color of Koryo is first under Heaven." Another Chinese gentleman, Hsu Ching, on a government mission to the Koryo court, was most impressed with what he saw and wrote about the beautiful porcelains at length. However, in general, they remained unappreciated outside of their own country until modern times.

While the "secret colors" attained in the Koryo celadons were indeed lovely and original, another quality that gave them a unique distinction not related to their earlier Chinese heritage was their shape.

Gourd and melon shapes were artistically enhanced by graceful, curved handles and spouts. Often these took the form of a twisted vine or a bent bamboo. Another typical form was a wine pot in the shape of a bamboo shoot.

Completely new was the inlay technique whereby delicate bird, flower, leaf, and vine designs were inlaid into the vessel body in black and white clay, and the celadon glaze applied over the whole.

The current value of Koryo celadons and their limited availability make them inaccessible to the average collector. However, modern reproductions, using the old techniques and quite fine in quality, are available.

Bottle. Inlaid celadon. Koryo period, thirteenth century. H. 12.5 in.

YI DYNASTY PORCELAIN

KOREAN PORCELAIN OF THE YI DYNASTY is widely varied in its decoration, design, and quality. As a whole it expresses a time of free forms, with an architectural quality in its shapes and a bold expressionism in its painting styles. These qualities give it a feeling of being extremely contemporary.

The Yi dynasty was a long one (1392–1910), and for the most part its wares are in great contrast to the preceding refined and elegant celadons of the Koryo period. The Koryo celadons are essentially aristocratic wares made for the court and nobility, while in the Yi dynasty a variety of stonewares and porcelains were produced for everyday use by the common people as well. The material was rough and sometimes crude, but the forms and decoration often possess a wild, free beauty rarely equalled.

In the early Yi dynasty, Koryo celadon died out and *punch'ong* stoneware, with its decoration of dipped or brushed white slip, was made extensively. White porcelain also made its first appearance. In the middle Yi period white porcelain flourished. It even gained fame and favor in China at the Ming court. At the same time *punch'ong* ware declined, and blue-and-white began to gain in popularity. In the late Yi period blue-and-white flourished and white porcelain declined. The Korean blue-and-white quickly achieved an entirely different effect from that of its Chinese inspiration. Designs were simple, and tones soft, giving it a faded, dreamy, poetic quality far removed from the precise and elaborate Chinese blue-and-white. The last fifty years of the Yi dynasty showed a great decline in ceramic production.

The Korean Koryo celadons have long been held in great esteem internationally to the almost total eclipse of the Yi wares. The Japanese have been the leaders in appreciation of the free form, naturalness, and vitality of the latter. They were especially appreciative of those pieces whose shapes could be put to use in the tea ceremony, for which their qualities are so perfect. Yi wares have also highly influenced modern Japanese potters.

There is a fair selection of Yi porcelains and pottery on the Japanese market today at prices that are sure to seem reasonable tomorrow, as these wares gain in international stature.

Vase. Blue-and-white porcelain, crane design. Yi dynasty, late eighteenth century. H. 8.5 in.

WATER DROPPERS—SUITEKI

ONE OF THE MOST INTERESTING accessories of the scholar's desk is the water dropper, *suiteki*, from which a few drops of water are used to wet the inkstone when rubbing the ink stick, called *sumi*, to produce liquid ink. *Suiteki* are usually closed containers with one or two tiny holes or openings from which to shake the water onto the inkstone. An earlier form was a small vessel on legs with a lid. Water was poured into this container and dipped out onto the inkstone in small drops with a tiny spoon.

Painting has been an integral part of Chinese culture from earliest times. It is believed to have been started at the beginning of traditional Chinese history (2697–2597 B.C.). Soon after, the first magical diagram was produced from which the art of writing is descended.

Painting and calligraphy in China might be compared with the tea cult in Japan. They held an important place in the aesthetic and spiritual life of the people. The scholar's desk and workroom, as well as his accessories, were given as much thought and importance as the action of painting itself. It was believed that an austere, tranquil mood had to be created in order for inspiration to flow into correct action on paper or silk. These traditions were assimilated into Korean art as well.

The material from which the water dropper was made and also its size and shape were very important.

The ink stick, too, was a matter of great concern, and most scholars had their own formulas for achieiving the best texture, scent, and color tone. The basic formula was made of carbon mixed with animal glue and then aged. Ink sticks keep for hundreds of years if enclosed in a box, and the older they become the more highly they were and are prized. Even today, Chinese *sumi* is considered far superior to that made elsewhere.

Korean water droppers are small art objects, fashioned in metal, pottery, or porcelain. They take many forms. Some are molded into animal and fish shapes. Fruits and flowers are also popular subjects. Geometric forms are often painted with figures or landscapes.

They are charming decorative items, can be used as desk accessories, or, when coupled with a small dish to hold water, make a delightful addition to a lady's makeup table.

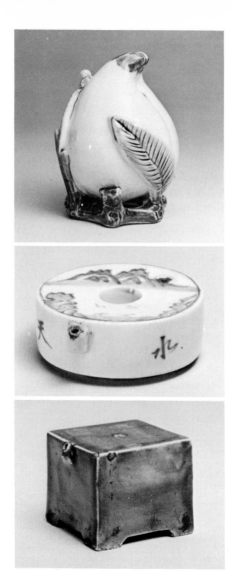

Water droppers. (A) Peach. Copper and blue underglaze on white porcelain. Eighteenth century. H. 4.75 in. (B) Blue-and-white porcelain. Nineteenth century. H. 1.75 in. (C) Underglaze blue porcelain. Nineteenth century. H. 2 in.

WEDDING DUCKS

THE KOREAN WEDDING DUCK is actually a wooden replica of a wild goose, which was part of a traditional Korean wedding. It was a ceremonial gift from the bridegroom to the bride.

This custom originated in ancient China with the ceremony of *chonan*, or marrying into the bride's family. It was the custom for the bridegroom to present a live wild goose to the bride's family. In return, the bride's family would send a pheasant to that of the groom. Both the wild goose and the pheasant were precious foods that could only be obtained by hunting, and therefore this ceremony of sharing such a delicacy was calculated to assure excellent family relationships.

The custom survived in Korea long after it was abandoned in China, and even today it is practiced. However, since geese and pheasant are almost nonexistant in modern Korea, the wooden duck is happily accepted as a substitute.

Wild geese and ducks have been symbols of conjugal fidelity and bliss in China and Korea from early times, since they are known to be devoted mates. In addition to the goose, other foods usually seen at Korean weddings are dates, symbolizing life and health, and jujube, a hard, strong fruit that is the symbol of the sons to be born.

Wedding ducks are usually carved in rather crude, folk fashion but have great appeal in their simplicity. This roughness is due to the fact that a man is supposed to carve only one in his lifetime. His personal traits are much more important in this matter than any ability as a craftsman. He must be a pure, honorable man, a good friend, and possess all of the Five Fortunes—traits shared by proxy with the newly wed couple. A possesser of the Five Fortunes must be wealthy, he must be in perfect health, he must have a family history free of divorce, he should have an obedient wife, and he must have lots of sons.

In the *chonan* ceremony, the goose, live or wooden, is wrapped in a red cloth tied under the neck, leaving the head and tail exposed. An older man with many sons is chosen to carry the goose to the bride's house. He is dressed in red, the felicitous color predominant at all wedding ceremonies. Once there, it is carried into the bride's room and put on the table where the couple share their nuptial cups. If a live goose should cry out during transport or, heaven forbid, escape, it can bring tears to the eyes of the bride, since it is considered an unlucky omen portending that the first-born child will be a girl. Of course, that is one great advantage in using a wooden replica.

Korean wedding ducks are appealing folk sculptures, and old ones can still be found in shops in both Japan and Korea.

Wedding duck. Carved, painted wood. Nineteenth century. L. 10.5 in.

TIPS ON ANTIQUEING

Regarding The Shops

Remember, this does not pretend to be a complete guide to all the antique shops in Japan (that alone would fill a volume). It is a selection of reputable, centrally located antique dealers carrying a varied stock "from soup to nuts." Some speak English and have contact with foreigners and the international market, while others speak only Japanese and rarely even see a foreigner in their shops. Many of the signs are written in Japanese only, but the shops can be easily located by following the map given for each district.

Merchandise

In most antique shops the merchandise varies a great deal from month to month, not to say year to·year. Therefore, do regard the following information as a general indication of the type of goods usually in stock.

Days and Hours

In many areas shops are closed on Sundays, however, not always. When the information is not included here, it is best to telephone before going, especially if you are on a limited time schedule.

Antique shop owners are generally late risers, so unless it is in the hotel arcades or larger shops, plan to start your antiqueing from around 11: 00 A.M. Many of the shops do remain open in the evening, however, until about 7: 00 or 8: 00 P.M.

Prices

While occasionally a note has been made to indicate price levels, no other price information is included due to the wide variance from shop to shop and the unfortunate but continuing escalation of prices in recent years.

Bargaining is not customary and often not understood in Japan. Therefore, in most cases the antique collector is expected to pay the fixed price. However, there are exceptions, and some shops will give a ten percent discount, especially to old customers. When prices run into the hundreds or thousands of dollars, there is usually some room for negotiation.

GUIDE TO ANTIQUE SHOPS

TOKYO

IMPERIAL HOTEL AND GINZA AREA

In the arcade of the Imperial Hotel are two antique shops that have enjoyed top international reputations for many years.

1. ODAWARA SHOTEN, INC., Imperial Hotel Arcade, 1-1, Uchisaiwai-cho 1-Chome, Chiyoda-ku, Tokyo. Tel. (03) 591–0052.

A favorite of local collectors, this shop carries Japanese and Chinese antiques, including screens, scrolls, textiles, lacquer ware, porcelains, woodblock prints, etc. The quality is from good to very fine and the English-speaking staff is friendly, helpful, and knowledgeable. They also do appraisals and packing and shipping.

2. MAYUYAMA & CO., Imperial Hotel Arcade, 1-1, Uchisaiwai-cho 1-Chome, Chiyoda-ku, Tokyo. Tel. (03) 591–6655.

This is a branch shop of the well-known main store and carries a small selection of top quality items, including paintings, lacquer ware, porcelains, sculpture and woodblock prints (see Nihonbashi).

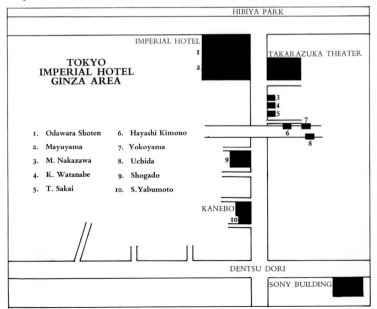

TOKYO IMPERIAL HOTEL GINZA AREA

1. Odawara Shoten
2. Mayuyama
3. M. Nakazawa
4. K. Watanabe
5. T. Sakai
6. Hayashi Kimono
7. Yokoyama
8. Uchida
9. Shogado
10. S. Yabumoto

3. M. NAKAZAWA CO., 14, 1-Chome, Yuraku-cho, Chiyoda-ku, Tokyo. Tel. (03) 591–2553.

Located on the street by the side of the Imperial, this shop has a good selection of woodblock prints, both old and new. They also have a branch shop in the summer resort of Karuizawa on the main street. English is spoken.

4. K. WATANABE CO., 14, 1-Chome, Yuraku-cho, Chiyoda-ku, Tokyo. Tel. (03) 591–2519.

Up the street on the left, here you will find a wide selection of Japanese antiques including Imari, lacquer ware, paintings, decorative bronzes, *netsuke*, *inro*, etc. Occasionally they also have Korean and Chinese art.

5. T. SAKAI, 1-14, Yuraku-cho, Chiyoda-ku, Tokyo. Tel. (03) 591–4678.

Established one hundred years ago, this well-known woodblock print gallery also has a branch shop in Kamakura.

Continue up the street, away from the Imperial, until you reach the INTERNA-TIONAL ARCADE on the left. Here you will find . . .

6. HAYASHI KIMONO, International Arcade, 4, 2-Chome, Yuraku-cho, Chiyoda-ku, Tokyo. Tel. (03) 501–4014.

This is the best place in Tokyo for finding old kimonos and brocade *obis*. They also carry second-hand wedding kimonos and a wide range of new *yukata*, *happi* coats, and all kimono accessories. They have a branch shop in the Hilton Hotel.

The next arcade is the SUKIYABASHI SHOPPING CENTER, also on the left. Take the stairs to the 2nd floor, where you will find two branch shops of Kyoto antique stores.

7. YOKOYAMA, INC., 2nd Floor, Sukiyabashi Shopping Center, Ginza-Nishi, Chuo-ku, Tokyo. Tel. (03) 572–5066.

A selective group of new and old paintings, decorative iron and bronze work, lacquer ware, Imari, etc. There are also branch shops of this famous Kyoto store in the Hilton and Okura hotel arcades. English is spoken.

8. UCHIDA, 2nd Floor, Sukiyabashi Shopping Center, 5-4 Ginza-Nishi, Chuo-ku, Tokyo. Tel. (03) 571–8077.

A discriminating collection of antique art objects, principally Japanese and Chinese, including woodblock prints, wood and bronze sculpture, porcelains and lacquer ware. English is spoken.

Exiting from the Sukiyabashi arcade, diagonally across the street you will find the Riccar Bldg. On the ground floor is . . .

9. SHOGADO, Ginza 6-2-1 Riccar Bldg., Chuo-ku, Tokyo. Tel.(03)571–0103.

This shop deals mainly in very fine Japanese, Chinese, and Korean ceramics and is well worth a stop for the discriminating collector. English is spoken.

10. S. YABUMOTO CO. LTD., 7th Floor, Gallery Center Bldg., 3-2, Ginza 6-Chome, Chuo-ku, Tokyo, Tel. (03) 572–2748.

Just up the street on the right, in a building on the corner past the Kanebo Department Store, this shop is one of the most famous in Japan for Japanese screens and paintings. They have a small selection of top quality art objects in view and a large stock from which to draw. Recommended for serious collectors, who might also like to visit some of the other antique shops in this building. English is spoken.

NIHONBASHI

This central area is located in the downtown shopping district of Tokyo and can be reached by taxi in a matter of minutes or by the Ginza Line subway.

1. TAKASHIMAYA DEPARTMENT STORE, Nihonbashi, Tokyo. Tel. (03) 211–4111.

One of the largest and best stocked department stores in Tokyo, Takashimaya has an Antique Section in the basement immediately adjacent to their Garden Department. Ask for *kotohin* (ko-toe-heen).

Here you can find a varied selection of predominantly Japanese and some Chinese antiques. Furniture, screens, porcelains, lacquer ware, bronzes, woodblock prints, scrolls, and many other items are on display. Prices are always in line with the current market value, and sometimes a real find can be made. Takashimaya is open on Sundays, when many other antique shops are closed, and American Express and Bank America cards are accepted.

FOR SERIOUS COLLECTORS
There is a group of antique shops in this area that deal mainly with other international dealers, museums, and collectors interested in top-quality pieces at current market values.

2. THE FUGENDO CO. LTD., 1, Tori 3-Chome, Nihonbashi, Chuo-ku, Tokyo. Tel. (03) 271–6671

Oriental arts including bronzes, sculpture, paintings, etc. and specializing in ceramics.

3. KOCHUKYO CO. LTD., 1-Tori 3-Chome, Nihonbashi, Chuo-ku, Tokyo. Tel. (03) 271–1835.

Just across the street from the side entrance to Takashimaya, this is one of Japan's top dealers in Chinese ceramics, also Korean and Japanese porcelains and other Oriental art objects.

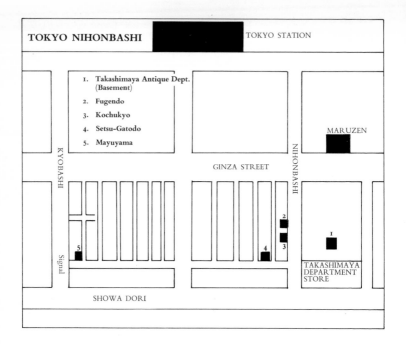

TOKYO NIHONBASHI   TOKYO STATION

1. Takashimaya Antique Dept. (Basement)
2. Fugendo
3. Kochukyo
4. Setsu-Gatodo
5. Mayuyama

KYOBASHI

GINZA STREET

NIHONBASHI

MARUZEN

Signal

5

4

3

2

1

TAKASHIMAYA DEPARTMENT STORE

SHOWA DORI

4. SETSU GATODO CO. LTD., 3-Tori 3-Chome, Nihonbashi, Chuo-ku, Tokyo. Tel. (03) 271-7571.

Japanese arts including pottery, porcelain, lacquer ware, sculpture, screens and scrolls.

5. MAYUYAMA & CO. LTD., 11-2-Chome, Kyobashi, Chuo-ku, Tokyo. Tel. (03) 561-5146.

Internationally famous, this shop is a must for the collector who desires quality. There is a wide range of Oriental antiquities from which to choose, from Japanese and Chinese porcelains, ancient pottery and sculpture to screens and scroll paintings, etc. The atmosphere is cordial and English is spoken.

HOTEL OKURA AREA

MILDRED WARDER LTD., Hotel Okura, New Bldg. Arcade. Tel. (03) 585-8274. Main Shop: 8-5, Kamiosaki 3-Chome, Shinagawa-ku, Tokyo. Tel. (03) 445-8901.

Miss Warder has a distinctive and appealing selection of Oriental antiques in her arcade gallery, including fine porcelains, lacquer ware, paintings, furniture and sculpture. Her interior decorating and furniture businesses are located at the main shop.

YOKOYAMA, INC., Hotel Okura, Old Bldg. Arcade. Tel. (03) 582-0111 Ex. 174.

A variety of old paintings, prints, lacquer ware, Imari, decorative bronzes, furniture, and personal accessories can be found here in addition to charming modern glass flowers and Japanese writing paper and cards.

Follow the street separating the Okura's old and new buildings along the wall behind the American Embassy and take the first street to the right. On the left you will find . . .

THE GALLERY, 11-6, Akasaka 1-Chome, Minato-ku, Tokyo. Tel. (03) 585-5019.

A jewel of a gallery and one of the local favorites, there is a wide assortment of Asian antiquities on hand from which to choose. Oriental rugs, ceramics, furniture, paintings, screens, sculpture, textiles, jewelry, bronzes, etc. Both decorative and fine art, not to be missed. Proprietress Julie Cohen also owns a shop by the same name in Palos Verdes Estates, California. Tel. (213) 375-2212.

Walk past the front of the American Embassy away from the Okura, turn left up the next narrow street and walk straight ahead into . . .

HARUMI ANTIQUES, 1-11-40 Akasaka, Minato-ku, Tokyo. Tel. (03) 585-0096.

This shop is an old house filled with a vast selection of antique chests, hibachis, Imari porcelains, folk art, paintings, woodblock prints, textiles, lacquer ware, dolls, etc. Owners Dave and Harumi Rose are hospitable and make shopping a pleasure. Good for gifts as well as collectors items.

In this same general area is the home and studio of . . .

MICHAEL DUNN, 3-21-4 Azabudai, Minato-ku, Tokyo. Tel. (03) 583-5933.

Mr. Dunn has an interesting selection of Japanese and Korean chests, Japanese porcelain, pottery, paintings, and metalwork and a wonderful array of baskets, all chosen with excellent taste. Well worth a visit.

SHIBA

Only a short taxi ride from the major hotels is a street called TOMOE-CHO, *which runs between the intersections of Toranomon and Kamiyacho. This street is parallel with Hibiya-dori on its way towards Tokyo Tower. It is lined with antique shops, and a leisurely walk can sometimes uncover an unexpected treasure. Most shops are closed on Sundays.*

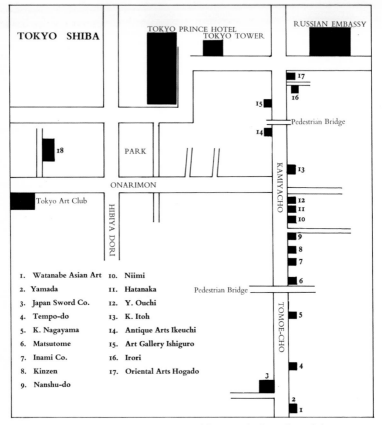

TOKYO SHIBA

TOKYO PRINCE HOTEL
TOKYO TOWER

RUSSIAN EMBASSY

17

16

15

Pedestrian Bridge

14

18

PARK

KAMIYACHO

13

ONARIMON

Tokyo Art Club

HIBIYA DORI

12

11

10

9

8

7

6

Pedestrian Bridge

TOMOE-CHO

5

3

4

2

1

1. **Watanabe Asian Art**
2. **Yamada**
3. **Japan Sword Co.**
4. **Tempo-do**
5. **K. Nagayama**
6. **Matsutome**
7. **Inami Co.**
8. **Kinzen**
9. **Nanshu-do**
10. **Niimi**
11. **Hatanaka**
12. **Y. Ouchi**
13. **K. Itoh**
14. **Antique Arts Ikeuchi**
15. **Art Gallery Ishiguro**
16. **Irori**
17. **Oriental Arts Hogado**

1. WATANABE ASIAN ART, Mori Bldg., 11 Akefune-cho, Shiba, Minato-ku, Tokyo. (03) 591–4527.

Several blocks from Toranomon crossing, on the right, Korean furniture and porcelain, Chinese porcelain, and Japanese ceramics and lacquer are some of the specialties of this shop. Some English spoken.

2. YAMADA, 11 Akefune-cho, Shiba, Minato-ku, Tokyo. Tel. (03) 580–7594.

Next door, this shop features Japanese porcelain, scrolls, and other art objects connected with the tea ceremony.

3. JAPAN SWORD CO., LTD., 81 Tomoe-cho, Shiba, Minato-ku, Tokyo. Tel. (03) 434–4321. Cable "SWORD" Tokyo.

At the next corner, on the left, is this shop famed for its old swords and sword accessories—*menuki, tsuba, kozuka*, etc.

4. TENPO-DO, 14 Tomoe-cho, Shiba, Minato-ku, Tokyo. Tel. (03) 431–3210.

Back on the right, this shop has a selection of Korean, Japanese and Chinese art, including porcelain, paintings, sculpture, and lacquer ware. The owner, Mr. Niwa, speaks English.

5. K. NAGAYAMA (ONKODO CO. LTD.), 20, Nishikubo Tomoe-cho, Shiba, Tokyo. Tel. (03) 431–0011.

Further up the street on the right; this shop has a good selection of Japanese and Chinese porcelain in a wide price range, depending on age and quality. They also have other items including lacquer ware and screens. A family business, the son speaks some English.

6. MATSUTOME CO., 42 Tomoe-cho, Shiba, Minato-ku, Tokyo. Tel. (03) 431–0725.

Up the street, past the overhead walk, still on the right is this shop specializing in tea ceremony utensils. This includes top-quality porcelain and pottery as well as screens, scrolls, and lacquer ware. English is spoken.

7. THE INAMI & CO. LTD., 42 Tomoe-cho, Shiba, Minato-ku, Tokyo. Tel. (03) 431–0640.

This shop specializes in Japanese swords and accessories. English is spoken.

8. KINZEN CO. LTD., 41, Tomoe-cho, Nishikubo, Shiba, Minato-ku, Tokyo. Tel. (03) 431–0633.

Another shop featuring tea ceremony equipment, this company has been in business for more than one hundred years. Tiny incense boxes in porcelain, pottery, and lacquer and hanging scrolls are some of the accessories they carry that are an integral part of the tea ceremony ritual.

9. NANSHU-DO CO. LTD., 41 Tomoe-cho, Shiba, Minato-ku, Tokyo. Tel. (03) 431–0645.

This shop has a wide selection of Imari porcelain and chests in addition to miscellaneous other folk and fine art. The owner, Mr. Makino, speaks English.

10. NIIMI SANKODO, 41 Tomoe-cho, Shiba, Minato-ku, Tokyo. Tel. (03) 432–1358.

Another family enterprise, the younger Mr. Niimi speaks English and is most helpful and knowledgeable about his goods. Chinese and Japanese antiques with some interesting Han dynasty inlaid belt hooks and old bronze mirrors are sometimes among the stock. A good place for the more serious collector.

11. HATANAKA CO. LTD., 38 Tomoe-cho, Shiba, Minato-ku, Tokyo. Tel. (03) 431–1003.

Something for everyone, good for more casual collectors who love to browse is this shop with a serendipity of merchandise. Folk items, chests, hibachis, smoking boxes, porcelains, Korean ceramics, blue-and-white Imari, Meiji glass, lacquer ware, etc. The owners are friendly and speak English.

12. Y. OUCHI, 2 Kamiya-cho, Shiba, Minato-ku, Tokyo. Tel. (03) 433–6036.
A shop featuring *netsuke* and porcelains.

13. K. ITOH, 28 Kamiya-cho, Shiba, Minato-ku, Tokyo. Tel. (03) 433–6064.
This shop has Japanese and Chinese porcelain and assorted other items. Mr. Itoh is kind and friendly and speaks a little English.

Cross the street at the signal by the Itoh shop and continue up the street until you find two shops on the left.

14. ANTIQUE ARTS IKEUCHI, 28 Yahata-cho, Shiba Nishikubo, Minato-ku, Tokyo. Tel. (03) 432–0012.
Again the implements and artifacts connected with the tea ceremony are carried here. This includes Japanese and Korean pottery and porcelains.

15. ART GALLERY ISHIGURO, 25 Hachiman-cho, Shiba Nishikubo, Minato-ku, Tokyo. Tel. (03) 436–1737.
This shop features good to fine quality Japanese porcelains with some Chinese and Korean pieces. A good place for more serious porcelain fans.

16. IRORI, 1-7-4 Azabudai, Minato-ku, Tokyo. Tel. (03) 586–8105.
An interesting small shop filled with folk arts including chests, textiles, porcelains, clocks and other decorative accessories. A branch shop is located in Kojimachi. Tel. 264–8654, Mr. Hasebe.

17. ORIENTAL ARTS HOGADO, 1-10-6, Azabudai, Shiba, Minato-ku, Tokyo. Tel. (03) 584–5558.
In the next block is this shop of top quality Korean, Chinese, and Japanese ceramics. Again, better for the more serious collector.

FOR SCREENS AND PAINTINGS

A few blocks away and very near the TOKYO ART CLUB, where antique sales are open to the public several times a year is . . .

18. HEISANDO, 13, 5-Gochi, Shiba Park, Minato-ku, Tokyo. Tel. (03) 434–0588.
This well-known and reputable shop has one of the largest and finest selections of screens and scroll paintings in Tokyo. They also carry ceramics, lacquer ware, etc. Definitely worth a visit for Japanese and Chinese painting devotees.

ROPPONGI

Approximately ten to fifteen minutes away from the heart of the city and most hotels, this area is easily reached by taxi and public transportation. Between the large intersection called TAMEIKE and the ROPPONGI crossing, the main street is dotted with antique shops. Begin across the street from the U.S. Trade Center at . . .

1. KOKADO, 1-4-18, Akasaka, Minato-ku, Tokyo. Tel. (03) 583–1619.
An assortment of Japanese antiques including lacquer, porcelain, screens, scrolls, etc. A small, friendly shop. No English spoken, prices moderate.

2. NAGANO, 23-4, 2-Chome, Akasaka, Minato-ku, Tokyo. Tel. (03) 583–4379.
Around the next corner and on the right side of the main street, this is a shop with a discriminating selection of temple sculpture, Japanese porcelain, lacquer ware, etc. Good to top quality at current prices.

3. NANBANDO, INC., 3-8, 2-Chome, Roppongi, Minato-ku, Tokyo. Tel. (03) 583–4558.
Continuing up the street, on the right, this is an interesting shop for both the beginning and more serious collector. It features a good deal of Japanese and Chinese porcelain as well as *netsuke* and miscellaneous other art objects. The father and son proprietors are hospitable and speak some English.

Cross to the left side of the street at the next signal with cross-walk and you will find . . .

4. KOJIDO . . . .
A shop with Korean paintings and porcelains as well as other Japanese and Oriental art objects.

5. TENROKUDO, 4-36, Roppongi 3-Chome, Minato-ku, Tokyo. Tel. (03) 584–3880.
This shop specializes in Korean, Chinese and Japanese porcelains of good to fine quality.

6. HONMA ANTIQUES, 5-1, 3-Chome, Roppongi, Minato-ku, Tokyo. Tel. (03) 583–2950.
A store with a varied selection and one of the favorites of local collectors. Japanese and Chinese porcelains and lacquer wares are some of their specialities. They also have a nice selection of small bronzes and a few top-quality screens and paintings. Interesting for browsing with good value for the quality represented.

(For those interested in modern Japanese pottery, on the right is TSUKAMOTO, a shop carrying Mashiko pottery and folkcrafts.)

7. KOTAKE ANTIQUES (HORYU-DO), 10-1, 3-Chome Roppongi, Minato-ku, Tokyo. Tel. (03) 402–4246.

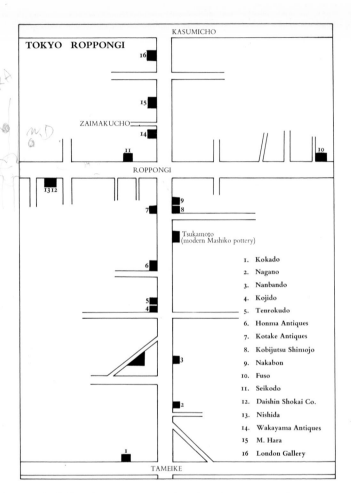

TOKYO ROPPONGI

KASUMICHO

ZAIMAKUCHO

ROPPONGI

Tsukamoto
(modern Mashiko pottery)

1. Kokado
2. Nagano
3. Nanbando
4. Kojido
5. Tenrokudo
6. Honma Antiques
7. Kotake Antiques
8. Kobijutsu Shimojo
9. Nakabon
10. Fuso
11. Seikodo
12. Daishin Shokai Co.
13. Nishida
14. Wakayama Antiques
15. M. Hara
16. London Gallery

TAMEIKE

Continue up the hill to the next signal and on the left you will find this shop, which carries an interesting selection of colored Imari and blue-and-white porcelain, woodblock prints, lacquer ware, decorative metal objects, etc.

8. KOBIJUTSU SHIMOJO, Nichiei Bldg. 1st Floor. 8-3, 4-Chome, Roppongi, Minato-ku, Tokyo. Tel. (03) 401–8460.

On the right, this shop deals in top-quality Oriental arts, including Chinese Han and T'ang figures and Chinese and Japanese porcelains. Interesting for serious collectors.

9. NAKABON, 8-3, 4-Chome, Roppongi, Minato-ku, Tokyo. Tel. (03) 408-1729.

Next door, this shop is owned by Mr. Nakajima, who speaks English and is most cordial and helpful with explanations regarding his stock. Japanese, Chinese, and Korean porcelains, lacquer ware, paintings, and sculpture from moderate prices up.

10. FUSO, 3-13, 7-Chome, Roppongi, Minato-ku, Tokyo. Tel. (03) 408-5510.

Four blocks to the right from Roppongi crossing, this shop is interesting for the average collector, especially those interested in chests, hibachis, and folk-crafts. Two floors are crammed with Orientalia, including paintings, lacquer ware, screens, Imari, personal accessories, lanterns, etc. A good place to browse with a broad price range. English is spoken.

11. SEIKODO CO., LTD. 1-6, 5-Chome, Roppongi, Minato-ku, Tokyo. Tel. (03) 401-8017.

Not far from the Roppongi intersection and a few yards from Goto Florists, this shop specializes in good to fine quality Chinese ceramics, including Han and T'ang figures as well as porcelains and bronzes. They also carry Japanese porcelains. Interesting for the more serious collector. English is spoken.

12. DAISHIN SHOKAI CO., 3-15-18 Roppongi, Minato-ku, Tokyo. Tel. (03) 583-2081.

About four blocks to the left from Roppongi crossing is this shop of Oriental potpourri: folkcrafts, objects of household use including porcelains, chests, hibachis, smoking boxes, and a good selection of old clocks. A family enterprise. The son speaks English, but is often away. Good for browsing and and an occasional find.

13. NISHIDA, 3-15-18 Roppongi, Minato-ku, Tokyo. Tel. (03) 583-6226.

Next door, this shop carries a small but discriminating selection of porcelains, bronze lanterns, lacquer ware, paintings, etc.

14. WAKAYAMA ANTIQUES, 2-22 Roppongi 6-Chome, Minato-ku, Tokyo. (03) 408-5969.

Back on the main Roppongi street, past the intersection and on the left, this shop carries antiques of high quality including Japanese, Chinese and Korean porcelain, paintings, lacquer ware, *netsuke* and *inro*. English is spoken. Interesting for collectors.

15. M. HARA, 23-1, 3-Chome, Nishi-Azabu, Minato-ku, Tokyo. Tel. (03) 408-0124.

Across the next intersection on the left is this shop, a bazaar of Japanese porcelains and many other items. Interesting for browsing.

16. LONDON GALLERY, LTD., Umeda Bldg., 3-20-14, Nishi-Azabu, Minato-ku, Tokyo. Tel. (03) 405-0168.

Down the hill, on the left, is this gallery of Oriental antiques including Japanese, Chinese, and Korean art. One of their specialities is Oriental porcelains, the other swords and sword fittings such as *menuki* and *tsuba*. They also carry Buddhist sculpture and paintings and European antiques. From good to fine quality. For the serious collector. English is spoken.

AOYAMA

Just a few blocks up the street from Roppongi, on a fork to the right, is the Minami Aoyama area and another group of antique shops. Also on this street is the small but excellent NEZU MUSEUM, surrounded by lovely gardens. Their Chinese bronze collection is known internationally, and one of the famous iris screens by Korin is in their collection.

1. SHIBUYA ANTIQUES, 7-1-3 Minami Aoyama, Minato-ku, Tokyo. Tel. (03) 407-1243.

On the left just beyond the signal where you turn right onto the main Minami Aoyama street, is this small shop loaded with bric-a-brac. This includes furniture, glassware, Imari, lacquer ware, etc. Fun for browsing.

2. ERAKU-DO, 6-21, 6-Chome, Minami Aoyama, Minato-ku, Tokyo. Tel. (03) 407-5694.

On the right side of the street this shop has an excellent selection of good to

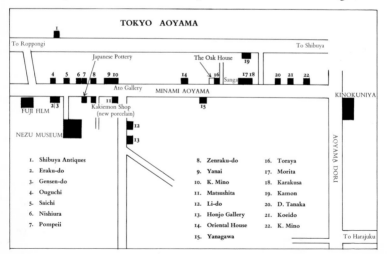

TOKYO AOYAMA

1. Shibuya Antiques	8. Zenraku-do	16. Toraya
2. Eraku-do	9. Yanai	17. Morita
3. Gensen-do	10. K. Mino	18. Karakusa
4. Ouguchi	11. Matsushita	19. Kamon
5. Saichi	12. Li-do	20. D. Tanaka
6. Nishiura	13. Honjo Gallery	21. Koeido
7. Pompeii	14. Oriental House	22. K. Mino
	15. Yanagawa	

fine Japanese and Chinese porcelain. Prices are reasonable for the quality offered, and English is spoken.

3. GENSEN-DO, 6-21, 6-Chome, Minami Aoyama, Minato-ku, Tokyo. Tel. (03) 409–7092.
Next door, this shop specializes in sword accessories and also has other Japanese, Korean, and Chinese art objects including pottery. English is spoken.

4. OUGUCHI, 7-2, 6-Chome, Minami Aoyama, Minato-ku, Tokyo. Tel. (03) 409–4603.
On the left, this shop specializes in Oriental porcelains but also carries some lacquer objects, sculpture, and bronzes. Moderate prices and up. English is spoken.

5. SAICHI ART CO. LTD., 6-7, 6-Chome, Minami Aoyama, Minato-ku, Tokyo. Tel. (03) 409–0600.
Across from the Nezu Museum entrance, this shop deals mainly in a good selection of Japanese screens and scrolls, but has a small selection of porcelains and lacquer ware as well.

6. NISHIURA RYOKUSUIDO, 8-3, 6-Chome, Minami Aoyama, Minato-ku, Tokyo. Tel. (03) 409–3751.
A few yards up the street is this shop specializing in Korean arts, including ceramics, paintings, chests, and folkcrafts.

7. POMPEII BIJITSU, 8-3, 6-Chome, Minami Aoyama, Minato-ku, Tokyo. Tel. (03) 407–2041.
Next door, one can find porcelains, lacquer ware, hanging scrolls, and other objects used in connection with the Japanese tea ceremony.

8. ZENRAKU-DO, 8-2, 6-Chome, Minami Aoyama, Minato-ku, Tokyo. Tel. (03) 409–5157.
Good to top quality Oriental porcelains as well as some screens and scrolls may be found here with prices commensurate with quality. Interesting for collectors. English is spoken.

JINTSU BUILDING, 11-3, 6-Chome, Minami Aoyama, Minato-ku, Tokyo.
This is a gallery of nine individual shops dealing mainly in top-quality Oriental ceramics at current market prices. Little English is spoken. With a few exceptions, most shops are not for the average collector but nice for window shopping.

9. YANAI GALLERY, Jintsu Bldg. 2nd Floor. Tel. (03) 409–5149.
On the second floor, this shop carries fine and folk art and is worth a visit.

Mr. Yanai speaks excellent English, is most cordial and very knowledgeable. His specialty is porcelain.

10. K. MINO GALLERY, Jintsu Bldg. 1st Floor. Tel. (03) 409–4318.

A miscellaneous selection of paintings, ceramics and other art objects from moderate prices up. Mr. Mino has a second shop further up this same street.

Next to the Jintsu Bldg. is ATO'S GALLERY, a shop dealing in European antiques.

11. MATSUSHITA ASSOCIATES, INC., 3-12, 6-Chome, Minami Aoyama, Minato-ku, Tokyo. Tel. (03) 407–4966.

Across the street at the signal, for woodblock print enthusiasts this is a must. Mr. Matsushita speaks excellent English, has one of the best selections in town of old prints (also some new), and some of the fairest prices. He is extremely cordial and knowledgeable in his field. Prices cover a broad range, from a few thousand yen up, depending on artist, quality, and condition.

12. LI-DO, 2-5, 6-Chome, Minato-ku, Tokyo. Tel. (03) 407–6420.

Across the side street on the left, this shop deals in Korean art, both new and old, mostly ceramics and sculpture.

13. HONJO GALLERY, Palace Aoyama Bldg. # 108, 1-6, 6-Chome, Minami Aoyama, Minato-ku, Tokyo. Tel. (03) 400–0277.

Further up this street, on the ground floor of the Palace Aoyama Building is this gallery dealing in old woodblock prints, Japanese screens, other antique objects, and modern art. Mr. Honjo is most hospitable and knowledgeable in the fields of art and antiques, and both he and his daughter speak English.

14. ORIENTAL HOUSE, LTD., 12-1, 6-Chome, Minami Aoyama, Minato-ku, Tokyo. Tel. (03) 400–0504.

For dealers only, and a few top collectors, this is the shop of Sammy Lee, well known in Oriental art circles and the author of *Oriental Lacquer Art.*

15. YANAGAWA ART STORE, 27-4, 5-Chome, Minami Aoyama, Minato-ku, Tokyo. Tel. (03) 407–2244.

On the right, in a modern building, this shop has screens, scrolls, lacquer ware, porcelains, sculpture, and a general selection of Oriental antiques. The owners are hospitable, and English is spoken.

16. TORAYA CO., 13-1, 5-Chome, Minami Aoyama, Minato-ku, Tokyo. Tel. (03) 400–8121.

A selection of Oriental antiques: porcelains, lacquer ware, chests, bronze wares, screens, scrolls, etc.

SANGA . . . .

Up the street on the left, this tiny shop deals in select porcelains, lacquer ware, and basketry, especially things for the Japanese tea ceremony.

17. MORITA, 12-2, 5-Chome, Minami Aoyama, Minato-ku, Tokyo. Tel. (03) 407–4466.

A favorite shop of local collectors for folk art and porcelains, there is always a good selection of noodle cups, basketry, Imari, some Chinese and Korean ceramics, Meiji glass, and wooden sculpture and furniture. Interesting objects at fair prices. English is spoken.

18. KARAKUSA & CO., 12-2, 5-Chome, Minami Aoyama, Minato-ku, Tokyo. Tel. (03) 499–5858.

This shop features a wide selection of Japanese blue-and-white porcelains, from sets of plates to small sauce dishes. Prices are reasonable.

19. KAMON ANTIQUES, 3-12, Shibuya-4-Chome, Shibuya-ku, Tokyo. Tel. (03) 406–1765.

Turn left at the corner past Morita's and left again at the next corner to reach this shop with an assortment of chests, wooden and porcelain hibachis, Imari ware, sculpture, screens, etc. A good place to browse. Prices are fair.

20. D. TANAKA, 11-5, 5-Chome, Minami Aoyama, Minato-ku, Tokyo. Tel. (03) 400–9550.

Back on the main street, Mr. Tanaka has a potpourri of Oriental antiques: Imari, lacquer ware, bronze wares, mirrors, and woodblock prints. Sometimes he has *Yokohama-e*, prints depicting foreigners.

21. KOEIDO . . . .

A tiny shop up the street on the left, the gracious proprietor, Mr. Nakashima, specializes in hanging scrolls, but no English is spoken.

SHIMBIDO . . . .

A few yards further, this shop also specializes in scrolls, but no English is spoken and most of the goods are not in sight.

22. K. MINO, 11-1, 5-Chome, Minami Aoyama, Minato-ku, Tokyo. Tel. (03) 400–9269.

Next door, this shop features mostly Japanese ceramics with some sculpture, lacquer ware, bronze mirrors, tea urns, etc.

The HARAJUKU shops are just five minutes walk from here (see map).

HARAJUKU

In the Harajuku area, about twenty minutes by car from downtown, there is a wide,

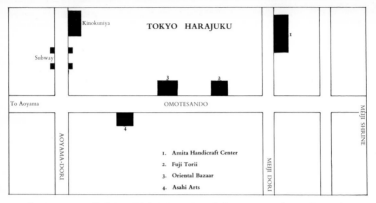

tree-lined avenue called OMOTESANDO and three antique shops of special interest
with one other just around the corner. The famous Meiji Shrine and Park are adjacent.

1. AMITA HANDICRAFT CENTER, 6-27-8 Jingumae, Shibuya-ku, Tokyo. Tel. (03) 407–9581.

For one-stop shopping, the new and old are combined here. Antiques include a very limited selection of Japanese porcelain, lacquer ware, *menuki* and *inro*, and a good variety of Japanese paintings and woodblock prints. Open daily from 10: 00 to 6: 30.

2. FUJI TORII CO. LTD., 1-10, Jingumae 6-Chome, Shibuya-ku, Tokyo. Tel. (03) 400–2777.

Both modern and antique Oriental art objects may be found. Old and new Imari, Kutani, lacquer ware, and other decorative items. Modern screens are sold here and special subjects are made to order. Closed Thursdays.

3. ORIENTAL BAZAAR, 9-13, Jingumae 5-Chome, Shibuya-ku, Tokyo. Tel. (03) 400–3933.

A vast potpourri of old and new, a great place to browse, both for gift items and an occasional antique treasure. Antiques include Imari, Kutani, lacquer ware, decorative metal work, chests, basketry, folkcrafts, screens, scroll paintings, wood carvings, etc. New items include stationery, ivory carvings, porcelain, lamps, bronze accessories, lacquer boxes, etc. Recommended as a real emporium, something to please every taste. Closed Thursdays.

4. ASAHI ART CO. Ltd., 3-10, Jingumae 4-Chome, Shibuya-ku, Tokyo. Tel. (03) 408–4624.

A well-known and reliable shop dealing in good to fine quality Oriental art objects. Sculpture, ceramics, gold lacquer, *netsuke*, *inro*, screen and scroll paintings, etc. Well worth a visit for beginning collectors to train the eye and for more serious collectors to check the current stock. Closed on Sundays.

Other shops of interest are . . .

JAPAN ART CENTER, Shinjuku, Tokyo. Tel. (03) 200–5387.

Located near Takatanobaba station on the Yamanote line, this shop features a potpourri of Oriental art including chests, hibachis, porcelains, screens, scrolls and folk art. Well worth a visit and Mr. Okada is both hospitable and knowledgeable.

TSURUKAME, Meguro, Tokyo. Tel. (03) 781–4523.

An old Japanese house filled with chests, hibachis, folk art, Japanese porcelains and Meiji clocks, a visit here is also a cultural experience as you stroll through the delightful nearby shopping street and enjoy the Japanese garden. Antiques of good taste and quality at reasonable prices.

KAMAKURA

KAMAKURA *is a charming little town located about one hour from Tokyo by train. It was an ancient capitol more than seven hundred years ago. Traces of past grandeur can still be seen in its temples and gardens, and the famous cast-bronze Great Buddha is here.*

Most of the antique shops are within walking distance of the station in a bustling area of mini-bazaars. The serious collector should bring an interpreter, for little English is spoken, The casual collector can manage, since the people are friendly and helpful with directions.

The shops can be located by following the map; their signs are usually in Japanese.

KAMAKURA STATION AREA

1. KAMAKURA ART (Kodai Bijitsu Ten), No. 2-10, 3-Chome Komachi, Kamakura. Tel. (0467) 22–1944.

Around the corner from the station (to the left) is a narrow shopping street called Komachi-dori. Up this street on the right is an interesting store that has one of the best selections of good and top-quality antiques in Kamakura. Objects such as screens, porcelains, lacquer ware, sculpture, and bronzes from Japan, China, and Korea. No English is spoken, and no credit cards accepted. For the more serious amateur and professional collectors.

2. SAKURAI, 8-10, 2-Chome, Komachi, Kamakura. Tel. (0467) 24–0860.

On the right, this shop features a limited selection of porcelain, including small objects such as incense boxes and water droppers and also some sculpture.

3. SHOJI SAKAI, 4-32, 1-Chome, Yukinoshita, Kamakura. Tel. (0467) 23–1049.

On the left, before the main junction, this shop deals in porcelain, *netsuke*, etc.

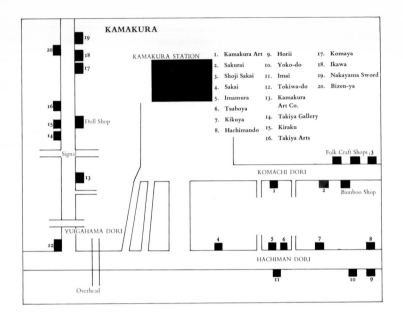

KAMAKURA

KAMAKURA STATION

1. Kamakura Art
2. Sakurai
3. Shoji Sakai
4. Sakai
5. Imamura
6. Tsuboya
7. Kikuya
8. Hachimando

9. Horii
10. Yoko-do
11. Imai
12. Tokiwa-do
13. Kamakura Art Co.
14. Takiya Gallery
15. Kiraku
16. Takiya Arts

17. Komaya
18. Ikawa
19. Nakayama Sword
20. Bizen-ya

Doll Shop

Signal

KOMACHI DORI

Folk Craft Shops 3

Bamboo Shop

YUIGAHAMA DORI

HACHIMAN DORI

Overhead

(*Also on this street are several folkcraft shops where gift shopping is ideal. Desk organizers, note pads and address books in colorful hand-made papers are inexpensive, light, and easily carried, and there is a wide selection of items including folk toys.*)

HACHIMAN-DORI

This is the picturesque street with its island of greenry that leads to the main shrine of Kamakura, the Hachiman Shrine. When exiting from the station, walk straight ahead until you meet this main thoroughfare, then turn left.

4. SAKAI, 2-11, Komachi, Hachiman St., Kamakura. Tel. (0467) 22–2100.

On the left, this well-known shop, established in 1874, features both antique and modern woodblock prints. The main store is located in Tokyo across from the side of the Imperial Hotel.

5. IMAMURA, 32-12, 2-Chome Komachi, Kamakura. Tel. (0467) 22–1347.

Continuing up Hachiman street on the left is a small shop full of bric-a-brac, including a small selection of hair ornaments, armor, porcelain, *netsuke*, and lacquer. Their specialty is old coins, paper money, and medals.

6. TSUBOYA, 29-12, 2-Chome Komachi, Kamakura. Tel. (0467) 22–8406.

This next shop has porcelain, including small noodle cups, temple furniture in lacquer, bronze mirrors, and other items. No English spoken.

7. KIKUYA, 1-9-22, Yukinoshita, Kamakura. Tel. (0467) 22–0615.

This shop does not welcome strangers, but if you speak some Japanese it is worth browsing through for an occasional find.

8. HACHIMANDO, 8-33, 1-Chome, Yukinoshita, Kamakura. Tel. (0467) 22-1568.

This shops carries old bronze lanterns, some porcelain, an interesting selection of bronze mirrors, *netsuke*, and *menuki* made into tie clips.

9. HORII, 7-12, 1-Chome, Yukinoshita, Kamakura. Tel. (0467) 23-1449.

On the opposite side of the street, this is a serendipity of discovery worth a few minutes' browse. Selection includes lacquer tea caddies, pewter saucers, altar tables, porcelain incense boxes, and many other small objects. Some English is spoken.

10. YOKO-DO, 12-3, 1-Chome, Yukinoshita, Kamakura. Tel. (0467) 22-2749.

This next shop has fine merchandise, concentrating on Japanese and Chinese porcelain, iron tea kettles for the tea ceremony, ancient Japanese pottery, basketry, and scroll paintings. No English is spoken.

11. IMAI, Hachiman-dori, Kamakura. Tel. (0467) 22-2983.

This shop specializes in dishes for the tea ceremony and also has a nice selection of varied antiques. Good for lacquer bowls, trays, and tea caddies, and sometimes a good scroll or screen painting can be found.

YUIGAHAMA-DORI

Walk straight ahead for several short blocks and after passing under an overhead bridge, on the right you will find another street lined with antique shops, YUIGAHAMA-DORI.

12. TOKIWA-DO, 2-Chome, Omachi, Kamakura. Tel. (0467) 22-6437.

On the left hand corner of the street is this shop with antiques ranging from folk pieces such as carved wooden hearth hangers from old farmhouses to good Chinese porcelains, with a varied assortment in between. This includes furniture, lacquer ware, scrolls, seals, sword guards, etc. Some English is spoken.

13. KAMAKURA ART CO. LTD., 1-3-2 Yuigahama, Kamakura.

Cross the railway tracks and continue up the street and on your right you will find this shop owned by Mr. Tashiro, who speaks excellent English. He is friendly and knowledgeable and has both Japanese and Chinese fine paintings as well as assorted other antiques. His prices seem very fair for the quality. A good shop for the serious collector.

14. TAKIYA GALLERY, Kamakura. Tel. (0467) 23-1209.

Continuing past the signal on the left is this small gallery with Chinese and Japanese paintings on scrolls and screens. A little English is spoken.

15. KIRAKU, Yuigahama-dori, Kamakura. Tel. (0467) 23–0506.

This shop has a potpourri of Japanese and Chinese antiques with some good porcelains. The price range is wide, from lesser priced items up to fine quality.

16. TAKIYA ARTS, 3-1-31, Yuigahama, Kamakura. Tel. (0467) 22–3927.

This large shop is owned by the same family as the gallery of the same name. They have a wide selection of Japanese and Chinese antiques, including Chinese (Ming) export ware, fine Japanese porcelain, scroll and screen paintings, sculpture, and lacquer ware. The quality is good to fine.

17. KOMAYA BIJUTSU-TEN, 10–6, Sasame-cho, Kamakura.

Several blocks past the signal light on Yuigahama-dori on the right side of the street is this small shop where the proprietor does not speak English but is very friendly. Objects include teapots in porcelain and iron, porcelain bowls, plates, etc., pottery, and lacquer. Quality and prices are low to medium.

18. IKAWA . . . .

This shop, just a few steps up the street on the right, is run by the son of the previous shop owner. It features miscellaneous items, but especially interesting are those crafted in wood. There are a few chests, hibachis, and smoking boxes of good quality.

19. NAKAYAMA SWORD & ART SHOP, 2-6-9 Omachi, Kamakura. Tel. (0467) 22–3167.

Also on the right up the street a few yards, is this store specializing in swords and their accessories such as sword guards and *menuki*. There is also a small selection of porcelain.

20. BIZEN-YA (I. Sawada), 3-9-33, Yuigahama, Kamakura.

Across the street on the left hand side is this tiny shop. The owner is knowledgeable and handles wooden sculpture, some fine lacquer pieces, and a few choice pieces of porcelain. No English spoken.

A DELIGHTFUL EXPERIENCE
THE HOUSE OF ANTIQUES 1449-24, Kajiwara, Kamakura. Tel. (0467) 45–1212.

Those interested in finer class antiques, especially pottery and porcelain, should not miss the home and studio of Yoshihiro Takishita. The house itself is a charming, two-hundred-fifty-year-old farmhouse of massive proportions, transplanted from Gifu Prefecture to the top of a mountain commanding a spectacular view of Kamakura and the surrounding area.

Mr. Takishita speaks excellent English and has a varied selection of Japanese antiques in addition to ceramics, including chests, screens, hanging scrolls, furniture, textiles, lacquer ware, etc.

He shows for a limited period of the month, weekends excepted, and by appointment only.

KYOTO
SHINMONZEN STREET

This is Kyoto's best-known antique shop area and is only a short taxi ride from the major hotels. Ask for Nawate-dori, Shinmonzen, and walk the length of the street (approximately three city blocks). Many of the shops are closed on Monday.

1. YOKOYAMA INC., Nawate, Higashiyama-ku, Kyoto. Tel. (075) 541–1321.

Located on Nawate-dori near the entrance to Shinmonzen Street, this is a well-known Kyoto store with antiques ranging from souvenirs to high quality merchandise. While they have a large variety of objects from which to choose, from furniture to porcelains and jade, their specialty is Japanese screens. They are familiar with the international market, do packing and shipping, speak English well, and maintain branch shops in Kyoto and Tokyo hotels. Most major credit cards are acceptable.

2. S. YANAGI, Nawate Shinbashi Agaru, Higashiyama-ku, Kyoto. Tel. (075) 561–5676.

Located across the street from Yokoyama, this shop caters to the Japanese trade and perhaps more serious foreign collectors. A range of Korean and Japanese ceramics are on display, with a few screens and scrolls in view. Not for the casual collector.

3. YAGI ART SHOP, 200 Shinmonzen St., Higashiyama-ku, Kyoto. Tel. (075) 661–7009.

This shop is worth browsing in for both the casual and more interested collector. Both Mr. Yagi and Mr. Usui speak English well and are most informative about the age and history of their antiques. There is a wide mixture of merchandise, a good deal of porcelain, both blue-and-white and colored Imari, and many smaller items. Specialities are *menuki*, *ojime*, and *netsuke*.

4. K. YANAGI, 231-2, Nishinomachi, Higashihairu, Yamato Taiji, Shinmonzen-tori, Higashiyama-ku, Kyoto. Tel. (075) 561–6067.

Next door to Yagi, this store has a selective display of porcelains, lacquer ware, and wood carvings. No English spoken.

5. RENKODO, Shinmonzen, Nawate, Higashiyama-ku, Kyoto. Tel. (075) 531–4586.

Continuing up the street on the right, this shop is only for the serious collector, since it handles only top quality pieces at current market prices, specializing in Japanese, Chinese, and Korean ceramics. The owner, Mr. Fukuchi, is most hospitable but speaks little English; an interpreter would be advisable.

6. MITURU AKAI, 231-1 Yamatooji-Higashiiru, Shinmonzen St., Higashi-yama-ku, Kyoto. Tel. (075) 541–6547.

This shop has a mixture of merchandise of varied quality: porcelains, basketry, lacquer, paintings and sculpture. Mr. Akai speaks a little English and is hospitable.

7. THE RED LANTERN SHOP, 236 Shinmonzen St. Higashiyama-ku, Kyoto, Tel. (075) 561–6314.

Across the river and on the corner of Shinmonzen and Hanami Koji, the next major cross street, is a shop considered to be one of the best in Japan for old woodblock prints. A mixture of old and new is available, and English is spoken.

8. G. NAKAJIMA, Shinmonzen St., Higashiyama-ku, Kyoto. Tel. (075) 561–7771.

Crossing the main street and continuing up Shinmonzen Street on the right is a shop of Japanese and Chinese antiques worth browsing through. Prices are moderate, quality is medium to good, and sometimes a find can be made. A little English is spoken.

9. K. KOTERA LTD., 245 Shinmonzen St., Higashiyama-ku, Kyoto. Tel. (075) 561–7770.

Across the street from Nakajima, this shop features good to top quality merchandise at comparable prices. Chinese, Korean, and Japanese furniture are their specialties. They also carry porcelain, paintings, and lacquer ware. Mr. Kotera speaks excellent English, American Express credit cards are acceptable.

10. F. MORISHITA, 245 Shinmonzen St., Higashiyama-ku, Kyoto. Tel. (075) 561–5585.

The next shop deals in Japanese chests and hibachis, and they have quite a large selection. No English spoken.

11. KYOTO SCREEN CO. LTD., Tel. (075) 541–2989.

This is a branch of the main shop further along Shinmonzen Street. See number 26.

12. OHHASHIYA, 239 Nakano-cho, Shinmonzen St., Higashiyama-ku, Kyoto. Tel. (075) 561–2968.

Up a few yards on the right is this shop of traditional Japanese musical instruments, both new and old. No English spoken.

13. Y. HIGUCHI, Shinmonzen St., Higashiyama-ku, Kyoto. Tel. (075) 541–6541.

On the same side of the street, this small shop offers Japanese Imari and Kutani porcelains, woodblock prints, and lacquer ware. No English spoken.

14. H. TANIGUCHI, 247 Nakano-cho, Shinmonzen, Higashiyama-ku, Kyoto. Tel. (075) 561–1371.

A shop of top quality that prefers to show only to museums and serious collectors. It has some sculpture, a few miscellaneous items, and specializes in *sumi* paintings. Good English spoken, but casual browsers not always given attention. Perhaps best to (have the hotel) make an appointment.

15. T. KITAGAWA, 248 Shinmonzen St., Higashiyama-ku, Kyoto. Tel. (075) 561–5802.

A shop with decorator pieces, baskets, lacquer ware, and a good selection of small blue-and-white and Imari porcelain objects.

16. RAKUYO SHOTEN, Shinmonzen St., Higashiyama-ku, Kyoto. Tel. (075) 541–4825.

A good place for decorative antique shopping, they have a wide range of items, from hibachis and Chinese lacquered leather chests to porcelains, lacquer ware, and a very good selection of smoking boxes. English is spoken, the atmosphere is cordial, and American Express cards are honored.

17. S. OKUMURA, Shinmonzen St., Higashiyama-ku, Kyoto. Tel. (075) 561–2385.

This shop, located on the next corner, specializes in carved ivory, *netsuke*, damascine, bronzes, and lacquer ware, both old and new. It offers a wide variety of merchandise, and English is spoken, American Express cards accepted.

18. K. IMAI & SON, 251 Shinmonzen St., Higashiyama-ku, Kyoto. Tel. (075) 561–0586.

Also on the left, this shop is located in a house more than one hundred years old. Their speciality is Japanese porcelain, especially blue-and-white, and they prefer to show only to serious collectors and museums.

19. T. IKEGAMI, 250 Shinmonzen St., Higashiyama-ku, Kyoto. Tel. (075) 541–4563.

On the right, this shop has miscellaneous items including chests, porcelains, and bronzes. Wholesale only.

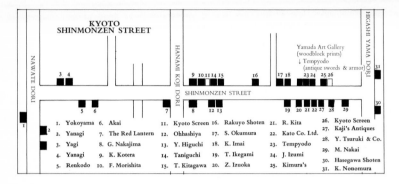

KYOTO SHINMONZEN STREET

HIGASHI YAMA DORI

NAWATE DORI

HANAMI KOJI DORI

Yamada Art Gallery
(woodblock prints)
↓ Tempyodo
(antique swords & armor)

3 4

9 10 11 14 15   16   17 18   23 24   25 26   31

SHINMONZEN STREET

5 6   7   8   12 13   19   20 21 22 27 28   29   30

1. Yokoyama	6. Akai	11. Kyoto Screen	16. Rakuyo Shoten	21. R. Kita	26. Kyoto Screen	
2. Yanagi	7. The Red Lantern	12. Ohhashiya	17. S. Okumura	22. Kato Co. Ltd.	27. Kaji's Antiques	
3. Yagi	8. G. Nakajima	13. Y. Higuchi	18. K. Imai	23. Tempyodo	28. Y. Tsuruki & Co.	
4. Yanagi	9. K. Kotera	14. Taniguchi	19. T. Ikegami	24. J. Izumi	29. M. Nakai	
5. Renkodo	10. F. Morishita	15. T. Kitagawa	20. Z. Izuoka	25. Kimura's	30. Hasegawa Shoten	
					31. K. Nonomura	

20. Z. IZUOKA, Tel. (075) 561–8872.

A small but cordial shop with a limited selection of lacquer bowls, trays, and some porcelain. A little English spoken.

21. R. KITA, 256 Shinmonzen St., Higashiyama-ku, Kyoto. Tel. (075) 561–6023.

A good and varied selection of old Imari and Kutani porcelains in a wide price range can be found in this shop. They also specialize in old *obis* and fans. English is spoken, and American Express and Diner's Club credit cards are acceptable. A must for porcelain buffs.

22. KATO CO. LTD., Shinmonzen St., Higashiyama-ku, Kyoto. Tel. (075) 561–1580.

This shop features old and new porcelains, carved ivory, bronzes, lacquer ware, and other curios. English is spoken, major credit cards accepted.

23. TEMPYODO, Uemoto-cho, Shinmonzen St., Kyoto. Tel. (075) 561–5688.

This shop specializes in antique swords and armor and also has one of the largest selections of Korean chests and furniture in Japan.

24. J. IZUMI, Shinmonzen St., Higashiyama-ku, Kyoto. Tel. (075) 531–4033.

Good quality merchandise and a few excellent pieces may be found in this shop. Woodblock prints, wood carvings, bronzes, basketry, scrolls, lacquer ware, etc., Mr. Izumi speaks good English and is most helpful and knowledgeable.

25. KIMURA'S ANTIQUES, Umemoto-cho, Shinmonzen Street, Kyoto. (075) 561–8871.

A shop specializing in bronze and wooden Buddhist sculpture. Also some Korean porcelain. No English spoken.

26. KYOTO SCREEN CO. LTD., 259 Umemoto-cho, Shinmonzen St., Higashiyama-ku, Kyoto. Tel. (075) 541–8785.

This shop specializes in screens and woodblock prints, both old and new. The Kawasaki brothers who own the shop speak English and are helpful.

27. KAJI'S ANTIQUES, Shinmonzen St., Higashiyama-ku, Kyoto. Tel. (075) 561–4114.

A large shop with a varied assortment of old Imari and Kutani ware, lacquer, bronzes, screens, scrolls, and various other curios. One of their specialties is screens, which are upstairs. The quality ranges from average to excellent, with prices to match. English spoken and credit cards accepted.

28. Y. TSURUKI & CO. INC., Shinmonzen St., Higashiyama-ku, Kyoto. Tel. (075) 561–1886.

A large store with good to excellent quality merchandise; one of the largest selections of screens in Kyoto, hanging scrolls, lacquers, porcelains, wood and ivory carvings, woodblock prints, etc. They also have a selection of Chinese antiques. Mr. Nakamura speaks excellent English, is most knowledgeable and helpful. Personal checks and major credit cards are accepted.

29. M. NAKAI, Shinmonzen St., Higashiyama-ku, Kyoto. Tel.(075)562–2906.

An interesting store in which to browse. Mr. Nakai provides antiques to many other stores, notably Takashimaya's basement antique section in Tokyo. He has a varied assortment of Japanese, Korean, and Chinese antiques including lacquer, porcelain, screens, scrolls, bronzes, etc. He speaks good English, and major credit cards are accepted.

30. HASEGAWA SHOTEN, Kitagawa Senbonnishiiru, Takatsugi-dori, Chukyo-ku, Kyoto. Tel. (075) 561–6653.

A real bric-a-brac shop with hundreds of small curios. Old watches, hair ornaments, prints, small boxes, dolls, etc.

31. K. NONOMURA, 291 Matsubaracho, Shinmonmae, Higashioji-dori, Higashiya-ku, Kyoto. Tel. (075) 541–3562.

A small shop with miscellaneous items, including porcelain and pottery, with prices moderate to low and quality of merchandise ditto.

SPECIAL EVENTS

If you happen to be in Kyoto on the 21st or 25th of the month, don't miss a visit to the picturesque TOJI TEMPLE (21st) and KITANO SHRINE (25th) outdoor markets.

Plants, goldfish, food, clothing, gifts, toys and many other items, including a few antiques are on sale. Try to arrive around 9: 00 a.m. for a leisurely walk through the grounds, since by 10: 30 one must push a way through the crowds.

At Toji, ask to go to the South Gate (Minami Torii), since the antique stalls are usually located close to that entrance. Prices are somewhat negotiable, and the merchandise ranges from low and medium quality to a real find now and then.

FOR THE SERIOUS COLLECTOR

YAMANAKA & COMPANY LTD., Awataguchi, Higashiyama, Kyoto. Tel. (075) 561–0931.

Don't miss a visit to one of the oldest and most reliable dealers in Asian antiquities. Well known internationally since early in this century, their main store is extremely large and deals with a wide variety of Oriental antiques priced from a few thousand yen up into the millions. Chinese and Japanese porcelains, stone sculpture, lacquer ware, bronzes, and screen and scroll paintings are among the items on display. English is spoken by all their staff.

Most taxi drivers are familiar with the name, otherwise ask for SHOREN-IN, which is a lovely temple located just across the street.

While in the neighborhood, drop in to . . .

ROBERT E. CURTIS LTD., 2-16, Sanjobo-cho, Awataguchi, Higashiyama-ku, Kyoto. (075) 561–2560.

Just down the hill from Yamanaka, here you will find Japanese and Chinese porcelains and bronzes, Korean ceramics, paintings, lacquer ware, etc. All from good to top quality.

SHOGADO, Oriental Arts–Curios, Anekoji, Kawaramachi, Higashi Nakakyo-ku, Kyoto. Tel. (075) 231–6626.

Another top-quality shop with a branch in Tokyo near the Imperial Hotel. A wide selection of Japanese and Chinese porcelains, bronzes, sculpture, and painting is available.

ONE-STOP SHOPPING can be accomplished at . . .

KYOTO HANDICRAFT CENTER, Kumano Jinja-Higashi, Sakyo-ku, Kyoto, Tel. (075) 761–0345.

Here you will find seven floors of Oriental arts both new and old, including porcelain, Noritake china, antique and modern woodblock prints, dolls, pearls, damascene, ivory carvings, cameras, tape recorders, silks and brocades and antique furniture and miscellaneous antiques. The antique furniture is located at the rear of the building on the 1st floor; the other antiques are in the UCHIDA ART CO. LTD. on the 3rd floor. Porcelains, screens, both old and new, hanging scrolls, lacquer ware, carved ivory and *netsuke* are a few of their specialties.

DINE AND ENJOY

A special treat at the Higashiyama Villa located just a few minutes from downtown Kyoto, but centuries away in atmosphere. Here you can feast on a traditional Japanese dinner, priced reasonably, in the lovely, serene atmosphere of a beautiful Japanese villa and garden. At the same time you can also enjoy a visit to ...

KYOTO ANTIQUES, Higashiyama Sanso, Higashiyama Driveway, Kyoto. Tel. (075) 581–3510.

Located on the same property and owned and operated by gracious Amy Takeda, the specialties here are chests, Imari ware, and lacquer ware housed in a centuries-old building.

The restaurant is open from 5 : 00 to 10 : 00 P.M. and the antique shop from 9 : 00 A.M. to 10 : 30 P.M. Best to call ahead for an appointment or reservation.

ALSO OF INTEREST

ON THE STREET running from the entrance to the Heian Shrine, pass the torii gate and art museum and in the next block you will find ...

HEIAN ART, Agaru Jingumichi Sanjo, Higashiyama, Kyoto. Tel. (075) 751–0277.

This shop has a wide range of antiques from hibachis to fine art in screens and scrolls. A fun place to browse, and young Mr. Fukumaru speaks excellent English.

NEAR GINKAKUJI, the famous "Silver Temple" is the home and studio of ...

MASAAKI UESHIMA, Tel. (075) 771–1197.

Mr. Ueshima shows by appointment and has an exquisite selection of Oriental antiques, including screens, scrolls, lacquer ware, sculpture, porcelain and textiles. Good for more serious collectors.

HOW TO RECOGNIZE, SELECT, AND PRESERVE ANTIQUES

LACQUER

Oriental lacquer is basically an organic "paint" made from the sap of the lac tree. Producing lacquer-coated objects is a painstaking process that requires dedication, skill, and patience.

Most items are coated many times with thin layers of this precious substance, and between the twenty to eighty or ninety coats, drying intervals of from two days to one month are required. Drying must take place in a cool, humid atmosphere for the best results. If the coats are not properly applied in dust-free conditions, discoloration, bumps, peeling, or loss of luster and smoothness will occur.

The production of lacquer ware has been a respected and cherished art in the Orient for over two millennia, always commanding top prices for quality pieces.

How to select

Good lacquer should have a high, healthy gloss. Look for cracking or peeling in the corners, joints, and on the edges of lacquer pieces. If this process has started, the object is a bad risk. If the wood itself is cracked, forget it, it is too often impossible to repair.

Remember that the lacquer coating cannot be successfully repaired without showing the mend, since the exact shade of the old lacquer cannot be duplicated. But if an object appeals to you, is priced reasonably, and can still be used as is (even with small surface chips from wear, or seams slightly pulling apart from expansion and contraction of the wood) by all means buy it and enjoy.

Tips on care

DO

- Wash lacquer in lukewarm water and *wipe dry* (bowls and trays).
- Wipe with a soft, lint-free cloth (preferably daily). Lacquer responds beautifully to such affection, and its luster will deepen with light rubbing. A *trace* of lemon or other light furniture oil in the wiping cloth is permissible.
- Store utility lacquer in a dark, dust-free cupboard.
- When storing good lacquer pieces, wrap them in a soft cloth or soft tissue paper and keep them in boxes.
- Use a humidifier in a room with lacquer furniture pieces or put

two bowls of water with a strip of gauze, from one to the other, nearby.

- Rotate lacquer pieces, "resting" them for a few months each year, preferably in the winter when the greatest amount of dry heat is being used.

DO NOT
- Wash lacquer in a dishwasher or use strong soaps or detergents.
- Let lacquer pieces accumulate dust.
- Use waxes or polishes on lacquer.
- Put lacquer in direct sunlight or near heat (especially central heating outlets).
- Spill alcholic drinks on lacquer.
- Put excessive weight or pressure on top of lacquered pieces.

Rewards

These cautions are meant to be gentle. The pleasure of owning good lacquer pieces is enough so that the few precautions for keeping them healthy are natural and effortless. Lacquer craftsmen relate to their material as if it is a living thing; owners of lacquered objects should do the same.

CERAMICS

Oriental porcelains have enjoyed great popularity from the earliest days of their production and continue to be admired and used by many. While the rarer porcelains of China and Japan are in a price category that prohibits their use, there are still many antique porcelains available that are not so highly priced as to be out of the question for special occasions or daily use.

While there are many types of ceramics, following are the general categories into which most fall.

Porcelain, often called *china*, is made from especially fine clays and pulverized stone. Bone china is a type of porcelain that contains bone ash in addition to the fine clay, giving it an especially pure white color. Porcelain is translucent, nonporous, highly chip and crack resistant, and when tapped, rings with a clear, bellike tone. It is fired at high temperatures, which gives it great strength.

Stoneware is made from less refined clays than porcelain and is usually much more thickly potted for durability. It is nonporous and stronger than earthenware but does not have the delicacy of porcelain, and therefore lends itself to rather bold designs, both in shape and decoration.

Earthenware is made of unrefined clays and is low fired. Therefore, while earthenware vessels appear to be much more sturdy than ones of porcelain, they are actually more likely to chip and crack, due to their porous nature and lower firing temperatures.

How to select

If you are "investing" in a fine piece of porcelain, pay the highest price you can afford for the best quality you can find and be sure the piece is in perfect condition with no chips or cracks. Of course, because of their rarity, some porcelains can command a high price even if they are slightly damaged or have repairs, but these fall into the category of museum and top collector pieces and are not in the price range of the average collector.

If you are buying porcelain for use, which is the most pleasurable way of owning and enjoying it, you should buy the best you can afford. However, a slight crack or a chip that is hardly noticeable or that can be repaired should not deter you if you like the piece, intend to use it, and the price reflects the extent of the damage.

One way of identifying old porcelain as compared to new is by the scratch or "use" marks, which are usually apparent on the inner face of the vessel, where utensils (ivory, lacquer, or wooden chopsticks) have left their marks.

Also there will usually be some fading or wearing away of the overglaze enamels in colored porcelains, although many were only used for special occasions. Pieces in which the colors are still in prime condition command top market prices.

The surest way of knowing what you are buying is to buy from a knowledgeable, reputable dealer. Should he inadvertently be in error, he will always be willing to buy the item back for what you paid for it. However, unless you are investing a considerable amount of money, (and therefore might like to take your purchase to another expert to verify its authenticity), the best plan is to develop your "eye" by comparing goods in various shops and then follow your own tastes and instincts. You can always sell or trade your purchase later (usually at a neat profit) should your tastes change.

The only way to learn the age and authenticity of various porcelains yourself is by study, both by reading and observing the finest examples in museums and by handling the porcelains themselves. It is important to observe the colors and patterns pertinent to a certain period, feel the weight of the object, note the color of the clay body on the bottom rim, how thickly or thinly it is potted, etc. This knowledge can only come with time and experience. Therefore it is important to rely on dealers in the beginning and always exercise your curiosity about each object to the utmost.

Tips on care

DO
- Wash porcelains in warm water and a mild detergent immediately after use. Food can cause spots and stains if left for any length of time.
- Soak porcelain overnight or for a few days in a mild bleach to help loosen and remove dirt and stains.
- Clean stubborn stains and cracks with damp salt.
- Clean dirty porcelain with a soft brush or cloth, using toothpaste.
- Use soft cloths or felt liners between porcelain objects when stacking to prevent scratches.
- Serve foods that require little or no cutting when using fine porcelains. The knife will make scratches on the surface of the porcelain and can also chip overglaze enamels.
- Repair favorite pieces of broken porcelain for home use by (1) cleaning the break surfaces thoroughly with the aid of a toothbrush; (2) allow to dry completely; (3) apply an adhesive carefully, removing any excess; (4) brace with tape, string, or rubber bands and allow adhesive to dry completely before removing.

DO NOT
- Hang cups from hooks. This will weaken the handles and eventually cause breakage.
- Use water that is too hot for washing porcelains. This can cause crazing (tiny, hairlike cracks).
- Use abrasives for cleaning porcelain with raised enamel decoration.

WOOD

There are many varieties of trees native to the Orient that produce wood of beautiful grain and texture. It has long been a tradition in the Far East to make the best use of the natural assets of each type by careful cutting, joining, and finishing so that the final object displays the most beautiful portion of the wood grain and is further enhanced by the high gloss, sheen, and translucency of the finishing process. It is also a custom to leave some woods in their natural, unfinished state. Japanese *kiri* is one of these woods that is cleaned and polished only by using fine sandpaper or steel wool on the surface and is left with a soft, natural finish.

How to select

There are many shapes and sizes in old Japanese *tansu* and hibachis as well as a large variety of woods from which to choose. Let your eye be your guide. You are sure to fall in love with something, and by all means that is the piece you should choose. The most important thing to remember about the condition is that first of all there should be no major pieces missing from the object, since these are almost impossible to match. Often various facings are used and many times glued on, so they are easily lost. The second point, in the case of *tansu*, is to check to see that the inside is in as good a condition as the outside. Often better woods are used for the outside of the drawers and a cheaper, thinner wood inside, which cracks easily and cannot stand the normal weight of clothing. Also check the back panel; it is almost invariably of thin wood and may be cracked. This, however, is easy to repair or replace in most cases. These points should affect the value of the piece. The state of the finish should be evaluated in terms of how much time and effort you are willing to put into it to get it into top condition. Many times a more reasonable price is possible if you are willing to do restorations yourself.

Tips on care

DO
- Dust often. Dust and dirt are enemies to a beautiful finish.
- When washing or refinishing, always test a small spot in an out-of-the-way place first to make sure the treatment will be successful.
- To clean very dirty wood, make a solution of one-half water, one-half ammonia, and wash, rinse, and dry the wood quickly in small areas.
- To clean off old wax and dirt, use a solution of one-third turpentine, one-third warm linseed oil, and one-third vinegar. For a smooth finish and to remove any stubborn spots, use the finest

grade polishing steel wool. Let the piece dry thoroughly (for two or three days) before applying wax. To keep *tansu*, hibachis, and other Japanese and Chinese furniture in top condition, this process should be done about once a year, since the old wax builds up, mixes with dirt, and the finish becomes somewhat cloudy.

- Use a hard wax, high-quality shoe polish in a compatible color on furniture regularly until you have built up a hard surface (perhaps 12–15 layers). After that, polishing with a soft cloth is all that is necessary.
- If wood has become very dry, after cleaning and before waxing, use olive oil and let it soak into the wood for a few days. Be sure that all traces of the oil have been absorbed before waxing.
- Clean any blonde or *kiri* wood with the finest-grade, polishing steel wool only.
- Use the pointed ends of hardwood chopsticks to replace missing wooden pegs in old *tansu*. Insert the tip in the peg hole, saw off, and whittle a new point to repeat the process.

DO NOT
- Use liquid waxes or furniture polish on Oriental antique furniture.
- Use any waxes, oils, or liquids on Japanese *kiri* wood. Only steel wool.

PAINTINGS

Japanese and Korean screens and hanging scrolls are often works of art that fit very well into contemporary decor and offer a constant source of enjoyment to the viewer.

The scenes are usually painted on either paper or silk, in color or in the traditonal *sumi* (black ink). Many of these works of art can be found in good condition due to the local custom of displaying scroll or screen paintings for a short period only to suit either a special occasion or the season. Otherwise they are carefully wrapped and stored away from light, dampness, and heat.

How to select

One's personal taste should be the main criterion in choosing paintings. Also, always buy the very best quality you can afford; your taste will only improve with time and experience, and any regrets will mainly be about what you *did not* buy.

If a considerable sum is being invested, be sure first of all that you are dealing with a reliable dealer and that the painting is in reasonably good condition. If repairs are needed, today's prices for this specialized type of work can often more than double the original cost. The dealer will be able to give you a close estimate of what the cost for repairs will be. On the other hand, something that is over one hundred years old, that has been used and enjoyed, cannot help but have a few nicks and scratches or whatever, and unless these have really damaged the painting itself, they should be accepted as a natural (and sometimes charming) part of the ageing process.

Some of today's best buys are in Japanese hanging scrolls, since few people take the time to unroll and look at them. They can be mounted in vertical frames and used alone or in groups to form a stunning picture wall.

Tips on care

DO
- Put tissue or soft, white paper between the panels, when storing screens, then wrap the whole screen in a cloth bag or heavy paper. Wooden screen boxes are ideal but rather impractical.
- Check behind screens in a damp climate to insure that mold or mildew is not forming on the back.
- Try to keep screens and scrolls in a temperate atmosphere. The greatest damage results from rapid temperature and humidity changes.
- Use a humidifier in winter and air conditioning in summer to keep the temperature stable.
- Air stored scrolls every three to six months to insure there are no insects in them and to allow them to breathe.
- Store scrolls by wrapping in a soft cloth or tissue and placing in a box (preferably wood). Rotate your paintings periodically, preferably every two to four months. This helps greatly in their preservation.
- Fold the two top tabs on a hanging scroll when rolling it up by creasing them at the top and folding them one over the other horizontally along the bottom of the top roller. When you hang the scroll, this will allow them to fall straight and not curl at the ends. The dealer will show you how to roll and secure the string on scroll paintings if you ask. This is a bit of a bother, but is an esoteric thing that is fun to know and do well.

DO NOT
- Put Oriental paintings in direct sunlight. Fading and damage to the paper or silk will ensue rapidly.
- Roll a scroll painting too tight or roll it off center and then try

to straighten it. This will only damage the painting.

●Display a screen where it is brushed constantly by people walking by.

●Try to clean or restore a painting yourself. This is a job for a professional.

WOODBLOCK PRINTS

Japanese *ukiyo-e* prints have been collectors' delights since the eighteenth century. They are a "people's art," mass produced principally for the middle-class merchants and tradesmen, who flourished in the lively and colorful Edo period in Japan. Finding their way to Europe via the trade ships, the flamboyantly colored prints also exerted a considerable influence on the nineteenth century paintings of the French impressionists.

How to select

There are many factors effecting prices of old prints. To evaluate whether a price is fair for a particular print, in addition to the overall composition and beauty of the piece, the following points should be taken into consideration.

1. *Classification.* The general, major categories of old woodblock prints according to their relative market value are (1) beautiful women, (2) landscapes, (3) flower and bird (limited production), (4) kabuki scenes, (5) warrior scenes, and (6) sumo wrestlers (limited production).

2. *Artist and Subject.* Even with the prints of such famous artists as Hiroshige and Hokusai, there is a gigantic gap in prices from one print to another, dependent upon the popularity or rarity of the subject depicted. Some prints by these artists can still be purchased for only a few dollars, while others run up into the thousands.

3. *Condition of the Print.* There are two points to consider regarding the condition of a print. The first is the original impression itself. The first or second editions are always more desirable than the later ones, since the impressions are sharper and clearer. Hiroshige often ran up to as many as fifteen editions from one woodblock. The second point is the actual condition of the print at the time of purchase. Trimming of margins, insect holes, fading of colors, dirt and foxing (brown spotting) all bring the market value of a print down. Almost all prints have some fading due to exposure to light. Since green colors fade most rapidly,

check the condition of the green in a print to get an indication of the overall color condition. Remember that a print by a well-known artist in poor condition is often less valuable than a print in top condition by someone less famous.

Tips on care

DO
- Frame your prints behind glass or plexiglass to protect them from air pollution, dust, and dirt.
- Make sure the framer is knowledgeable about prints and will use only paper and cardboard of pure rag content. Chemicals in some materials can be damaging to prints.
- Mat your prints, not only to enhance their appearance, but to hold the print away from the glass surface and allow air to circulate.
- Rotate your prints. Ideally no print should be displayed for longer than three months at a time. Then it should be rested in a dark, dry place. This will also keep your eye fresh and accelerate your enjoyment of the prints.
- Store your prints either in their frames or flat in a folder made of cardboard of pure rag fiber with no harmful chemicals.
- Air prints at least once every six months to check for insect damage and allow them to breathe, preventing mildew.

DO NOT
- Try to repair or clean a print yourself. Take it to a professional.
- Trim edges of prints in order to fit them into frames. This reduces their value drastically.
- Expose prints to direct sunlight. This will cause the colors to fade and deteriorate rapidly, reducing the value of the print.
- Put a print directly against glass or plexiglass. This will allow moisture to form and damage the print.
- Put mothballs in prints to keep insects out. The chemicals will turn the paper brown.

HELPFUL READING

ART HISTORY

Noma, Seiroku. *The Arts of Japan*. 2 vols. Tokyo: Kodansha International, 1967.

Tokyo National Museum Staff. *Pageant of Japanese Art*. 6 vols. Tokyo: Toto Bunka, 1952.

Shosoin Office. *Treasures of the Shosoin*. Tokyo: Asahi Shimbun Publishing Co., 1965.

Yashiro, Yukio. *Art Treasures of Japan*. 2 vols. Tokyo: Kokusai Bunka Shinkokai, 1960.

GENERAL

Feddersen, Martin. *Japanese Decorative Art*. Translated by Katherine Watson. London: Faber and Faber, 1962.

Bushell, Raymond. *An Introduction to Netsuke*. Tokyo: Charles E. Tuttle, 1971.

Fujiya Hotel, Ltd. *We Japanese*. Yokohama: Yamagata Press, 1950.

Joya, Mock. *Things Japanese*. Tokyo: Tokyo News Service, 1968.

Malm, W.P. *Japanese Music and Musical Instruments*. Tokyo: Charles E. Tuttle, 1974.

Minnich, Helen B. *Japanese Costume, and the Makers of Its Elegant Tradition*. Rutland, Vermont & Tokyo, Japan: Charles E. Tuttle, 1950.

Morse, Edward S. *Japanese Homes and Their Surroundings*. Tokyo: Charles E. Tuttle, 1972.

Muraoka, Kageo and Okamura, Kichiemon. *Folk Arts and Crafts Of Japan*. The Heibonsha Survey of Japanese Art, vol. 26. New York, Tokyo: Weatherhill/Heibonsha, 1973.

Nakamura, Yasuo. *Noh: The Classical Theater*. Performing Arts of Japan: IV. New York, Tokyo: Weatherhill/Tankosha, 1971.

Newman, Alex R., and Ryerson, Egerton. *Japanese Art, A Collector's Guide*. New York: A.S. Barnes, 1964.

Sakai, Atsuharu. *Japan in a Nutshell*. Yokohama: Yamagata Printing Co., 1952.

Wells, Florence. *Japanese Fans—History & Usage*. Tokyo: The Foreign Affairs Association of Japan, 1960.

LACQUER

Casal, U.A. *Japanese Art Lacquers*. Tokyo: Sophia University, 1961.

Jahss, Melvin and Betty. *Inro and other miniature forms of Japanese Lacquer Art*. Tokyo: Charles E. Tuttle, 1971.

Lee, Yu-kuan. *Oriental Lacquer Art*. Tokyo: Weatherhill, 1972.

Stern, Harold P. *The Magnificent Three: Lacquer, Netsuke, and Tsuba, Selections from the Collection of Charles A. Greenfield*. Catalogue of the Japan House Gallery. New York: Japan Society, Inc., 1972.

PAINTING

Awakawa, Yasuichi. *Zen Painting*. Tokyo: Kodansha International, 1970.

Grilli, Elise. *The Art of the Japanese Screen*. Tokyo: Weatherhill, 1970.

Mizuo, Hiroshi. *Edo Painting: Sotatsu and Korin*. Tokyo: Weatherhill, 1972.

Noma, Seiroku. *Artistry in Ink*. Tokyo: Toto Bunka, 1957.

Tanaka, Ichimatsu. *Japanese Ink Painting: Shubun to Sesshu*. Tokyo: Weatherhill/Heibonsha, 1972.

Tokyo National Museum Staff. *Pageant of Japanese Art*. Vols. I, II. Tokyo: Toto Bunka, 1952.

Yamane, Yuzo. *Momoyama Genre Painting*. Tokyo: Weatherhill/Heibonsha, 1973.

Yonezawa, Yoshiko, and Yoshizawa, Chu. *Japanese Painting in the Literati Style*. Tokyo: Weatherhill/Heibonsha, 1974.

POTTERY AND PORCELAIN

Garner, Sir Harry. *Oriental Blue & White*. London: Faber and Faber, 1970.

Gorham, Hazel H. *Japanese and Oriental Ceramics*. Tokyo: Charles E. Tuttle, 1971.

Jenyns, Soame. *Japanese Porcelain*. New York: Praeger, 1965.

———. *Japanese Pottery*. London: Faber and Faber, 1971.

Munsterberg, Hugo. *The Ceramic Art of Japan*. Tokyo: Charles E. Tuttle, 1969.

Penkala, Maria. *Far Eastern Ceramics*. The Hague: Mouton & Co., 1963.

Rhodes, Daniel. *Tamba Pottery*. Tokyo: Kodansha International, 1972.

WOODBLOCK PRINTS

Michener, James. *Japanese Prints, From the Early Masters to the Modern*. Tokyo: Charles E. Tuttle, 1959.

Narazaki, Muneshige. *The Japanese Print*. Adapted by C.H. Mitchell. Tokyo: Kodansha International, 1966.

KOREAN ART AND CUSTOMS

Bishop, Isabella B. *Korea and Her Neighbors*. Seoul, Korea: Yonsei University Press, 1970.

Folkist Society. *Folkism*. Translated by Carl and Jennifer Strom. Seoul, Korea: Emillle Museum, 1972.

Gompertz, G.M. *Korean Celadon and Other Wares of the Koryo Period*. London: Faber and Faber, 1963.

———. *Korean Pottery & Porcelain of the Yi Period*. London; Faber and Faber, 1968.

Honey, W.B. *Corean Pottery*. New York: D. Van Nostrand, 1948.

Kim, Chewon and Kim, Won-yong. *Treasures of Korean Art: 2000 Years of Ceramics, Sculpture and Jeweled Arts*. New York: 1966.

McCune, Evelyn. *The Arts of Korea*. Tokyo: Charles E. Tuttle, 1967.

Catalogue. *Masterpieces of Korean Art*. Boston: T.O. Metcalf, 1957.

Catalogue. *The Art of the Korean Potter, Silla, Koryo, Yi*. New York: The Asia Society, Inc., 1968.

GLOSSARY

AMAGAI JIZO	Rain-bringing patron saint.
ANDON	Lamp of wood and paper.
ANKA	An earthenware pot covered with a wooden grill, used as a foot warmer.
ARITA	A major porcelain producing district in Japan, located on the southern island of Kyushu.
ASHIYA-GAMA	Iron kettles produced in the village of Ashiya for use in the tea ceremony.
BANGASA	Umbrella of wood and oiled paper.
BANZUKE	Ranking lists published after each sumo wrestling tournament.
BEKKO	Tortoiseshell.
BIJINGA	Woodblock prints of beautiful women.
BINKAKE	Porcelain braziers.
BIWA	A stringed instrument similar to a lute.
BIZEN	One of the "six ancient kilns" famous for its pottery.
BLACK SHIP	A porcelain pattern depicting the Dutch ships and Hollanders in their native European dress.
BODHIDHARMA	Indian patriarch who introduced Zen Buddhism to China.
BON	Serving trays.
BON	A Buddhist festival for departed souls.
BON ODORI	A community dance performed in midsummer during the Bon (All Souls) Festival.
BUGAKU	Court dances using masks.
BUNDAI	A small reading table.
BUNRAKU	The puppet drama.
BUYO	A dance drama.
BYOBU	Folding screens of from two to eight panels used in Japanese buildings as room dividers, to reflect light, and to prevent drafts.
CELADON	Porcelains in a wide range of soft green and blue-green colors produced in many Asian countries, the earliest appearing during the Sung dynasty in China (960–1279 A.D.).
CHA	Tea.
CHABAKO	Box or chest used by merchants for storing green tea.

CHABIN	A teapot.
CHADO	The Way of Tea (the tea ceremony).
CHAEKKORI	Korean scholar's study paintings.
CHAGAMA	Teakettle.
CH'AN	Chinese name for the Zen sect of Buddhism.
CHA-NO-YU	Literally "hot water for tea," meaning the tea ceremony.
CHAYA	A restaurant or tea store.
CHITSU	Covers for sutra rolls made of cloth and bamboo.
CHIZU	Map.
CHOCHIN	Paper lantern used outdoors.
CHOKO	Saké cup.
CHONAN	A Chinese and Korean ceremony of marrying into the bride's family.
CHOSHI	A ceremonial wine pourer made of lacquered wood.
DAIMYO	Feudal lords of old Japan.
DAIWA-HIBACHI	Rectangular wooden braziers with a thick shelf surrounding the fire box. Made and used in the Kyoto, Kansai region.
DATE-MON	"Dandyish" crests used by merchant families.
DOBIN	An earthen tea pot.
DORI	Street or avenue.
EBIKO	A blend of incenses used for perfuming clothes.
ECHIZEN	One of the "six ancient kilns" famous for its pottery.
EDO-HIBACHI	Tokyo style wooden brazier with straight sides.
E-HON	Illustrated book.
EMA	Votive paintings on wood, often of horses.
FUBAKO	Letter box.
FUDE	Writing brush.
FUKU	Good fortune.
FUKU-CHA	New Year's tea.
FURIDASHI	Herb medicine.
FUSUMA	Sliding doors.
FUTON	Padded bedding placed on the floor.
GAGAKU	Court music.
GEGYO	Carved fish hung in the gables of temples and houses as a protective charm against fire.
GEISHA	Female courtesan, companion, entertainer.
GIGAKU	A masked Buddhist ritual, now forgotten.
GIN-MAKI-E	Silver decorated lacquer.

GINSENG	Korean root believed to have curative powers.
HAI-DAI	Saké cup stands made of lacquered wood or porcelain.
HAISEN	Cup washing stand or bowl.
HAKAMA	Skirt-like trousers similar to long culottes once worn by both men and women but now worn principally in the Japanese traditional theater.
HAKO-MAKURA	Pillow box of wood and sometimes leather.
HAMAGURI	A species of clam whose shells were used in the popular shell matching game *kai-awase*.
HAN	Seal or stamp.
HANA-AWASE	A game still played today involving cards picturing flowers.
HANAMI-JU	Portable food box carried along for flower viewing.
HANIWA	Clay figures with cylindrical bases stuck into the earth around grave mounds in the 3rd to 5th centuries.
HARIBAKO	Sewing box.
HARIBAKO-GIN	Literally "sewing box gold," a woman's secret savings.
HARI-KUYO	Religious ceremony for broken needles.
HASHI	Chopsticks.
HASHIBAKO	Box for a pair of chopsticks.
HASHITATE	Container for holding chopsticks.
HIBACHI	Wooden, metal, or porcelain charcoal braziers.
HIKITE	Recessed metal door pull on the Japanese sliding door.
HINA	A type of Japanese doll.
HI-OGI	A wooden slat fan.
HIRAMAKI-E	Designs in low relief on lacquer.
HIRAME	A lacquer process in which small flakes of gold or silver leaf are placed irregularly on a colored surface.
HON	Book.
HWAGAK	(Korean) Painted oxhorn.
IGA	A kiln well known for producing pottery tea ceremony utensils.
IKO	Clothing stand.
IMARI	Porcelain made in the Arita district, which was named after the port city of Imari from which it was exported.
IN	Seal or stamp.
INRO	Small, portable medicine boxes made up of tiers.

IRORI	Open hearth pit.
ISHI-DORO	Stone lantern.
JIZAI-KAGI	Hearth hanger.
JIZO	Popular patron saint, originally of small children, later of the common people.
JORURI	A recitative song-poem.
JUBAKO	Stacked food boxes in lacquered wood or porcelain.
KABUKI	Japanese popular theater of the Edo period..
KAGURA	"God music," the earliest form of Japanese music and dance performed at Shinto shrine ceremonies.
KAI-AWASE	A game of matching painted shells popular for many centuries among the aristocracy.
KAI-OKE	Lacquered boxes used to store painted clam shells used in *kai-awase*.
KAIRO	A small metal container to hold powdered charcoal. Used as a pocket or bosom warmer.
KAKEMONO	Hanging scrolls.
KAKE-SOBA	Noodles served in a soup.
KAKI	Persimmon.
KAKIEMON	A fine Japanese porcelain.
KAME	A tortoise.
KAMI-SAMA	Japanese gods of the Shinto religion.
KANBAN	Business and shop signs.
KANO	A school of painting begun in the mid fifteenth century that treated subjects in a monumental fashion and was one of the major schools of Japanese painting for many centuries.
KASHIHON-YA	Book-lending shops.
KASUGA	A shape of lantern, named after a famous shrine.
KENDAI	Reading stand.
KESHO-MAWASHI	Ceremonial aprons worn by sumo wrestlers.
KIKU	Chrysanthemum; the flower of sixteen petals is the emblem of the Japanese imperial family.
KIMONO	Literally, "clothing," also the traditional Japanese garment worn by both women and men.
KIN-MAKI-E	Gold decorated lacquer.
KINUMO	Silk cloth.
KIRI	Wood of the paulownia tree.
KIRIKANE	A lacquer process. Gold cut in tiny squares or strips and applied to small areas of a pattern to

	bring out a natural shading or enhance the design.
KIRI-SOBA	Buckwheat noodles cut in long strips.
KISERU	Small pipe for smoking tobacco.
KO-AWASE	The incense game.
KOBAKO	Boxes for holding incense.
KODO	Incense appreciation.
KOAN PICTURES	"Puzzle pictures" expressing the moment of enlightenment; used in the teaching of Zen Buddhism.
KOGAI	Skewer used for personal grooming, a part of the sword furniture.
KO-IMARI	"Old Imari," produced from around 1650 to 1750.
KOJIKI	Chronicles of Japan.
KOKESHI	Wooden dolls.
KO-KUTANI	"Old Kutani," an early porcelaneous ware produced from 1655 to 1704.
KOMUSO	A group of itinerate priest-spies of the Edo period (1614–1868).
KORIN	A leading painter of the Rimpa school of decorative painting.
KORO	Incense burner.
KOSODE	Ladies' inner robe that eventually was worn on the outside and became the modern kimono.
KOTATSU	Small hearth covered by a quilt under which a family puts their feet and legs to keep warm.
KOTO	Thirteen-stringed musical instrument somewhat like a harp.
KOZUKA	Utility knife carried as part of the sword.
KUGIKAKUSHI	Metal nailhead covers.
KUKEDAI	An upright appendage attached to the sewing box used to hold a pin cushion and to assist in sewing by holding the fabric taut.
KUROYAKI	Crane's legs burned to a medicinal ash, said to cure whooping cough.
KUSURI-DANSU	Medicine chest.
KUTANI	A porcelaneous ware produced in Kaga Province.
KYOBAKO	Sutra boxes.
KYODAI	Cosmetic stand with drawers to hold makeup and personal accessories.
KYOSOKU	Armrests made of wood with an attached cushion.
MAITREYA	The Buddhist Messiah yet to come.

MAKI-E	The art of applying gold and silver to lacquer pieces.
MAKURA	Pillow; of wood, porcelain, or straw.
MATSU	Pine.
MAYUZUMI	A mixture of lamp soot and sesame oil used as brow makeup by ladies of the Heian era.
MENUKI	Sword-peg ornaments.
MIDARE-BAKO	Tray or box for storing kimonos.
MINGEI	Folk art.
MISE-HIBACHI	Small brazier used in a shop to set before a customer.
MISHIMA WARE	Gray stoneware with "inlaid" decoration in white slip.
MIZUIRE	A small metal water container used in preparing black ink.
MOCHI	Glutinous rice cakes eaten especially at New Year's.
MON	Family crests originally used by the imperial court and the aristocracy. Business crests came to be used later by the merchants.
MORI-SOBA	Buckwheat noodles served with the sauce on the side.
MT. KOYA	A famous mountain retreat with numerous temples; the center of the Shingon sect of Buddhism.
NABESHIMA	A famous porcelain named after Lord Nabeshima who started the kiln.
NAGA-HIBACHI	Rectangular wooden braziers, popular in the Edo period.
NAGASAKI-E	Woodblock prints depicting foreigners of that port city.
NAGASAKI WARES	Porcelains in European shapes exported from the port of Nagasaki in the Meiji era.
NAGAUTA	A Japanese narrative song.
NASHIJI	A lacquer technique of speckled gold in which the finish looks like the skin of a pear.
NEGORO	A lacquer technique with applications of red lacquer over black.
NEGORO-DERA	A Buddhist monastery in Wakayama Prefecture where the first *negoro* lacquer ware was produced.
NEKO-ASHI	*Neko* is a cat, and *ashi* legs or feet. Usually this refers to a tray with gracefully curved legs.
NETSUKE	Toggles for money purses, medicine boxes, and tobacco pouches hung from the *obi*.
NIHON SHOKI	Chronicles of Japan. The oldest written history of

Japan, believed to be part fact and part mythology. Most of the dates given are considered to be at least two hundred years later.

NINGYO	Dolls.
NISHIKI	Brocade.
NISHIKI-DE	"Brocade wares"—highly decorated Imari porcelain with the design covering most of the vessel.
NOH	A poetic dance drama using masks.
NOREN	Curtains used in doorways.
NURIMONO	Objects coated with lacquer.
NYOBO SHOZOKU	Court dress of the Heian era consisting of twelve or more layers of garments.
NYOI	Buddhist sceptor.
OBON	Festival for the spirits of the dead.
OBUNKYO-NINGYO	Papier-maché receptacle dolls used to present gifts of food and sweets.
OCHANOMIZU	The name of a place with a railway stop in Tokyo, located beside a river once famous for its clear water used for the tea ceremony.
OGI	A Japanese fan.
OJIME	Bead, used with *netsuke* and *inro*.
O-JUKKO	Incense log.
ONIWA GAMA	Non-commercial "garden kilns," porcelain producing kilns on the private premises of the gentry. The ceramics produced were for the private use of the lord and his retinue and also given as special gifts.
ORIBE	A shape of lantern named after a tea master.
OSHOGATSU	New Year's.
OT-CHANG	Korean wooden chests.
OTOSO	New Year's saké prepared with spices.
OTSU-E	Folk paintings from the Lake Biwa region near Kyoto.
OZONI	Soup eaten at New Year's.
PO SHAN LU	Chinese incense burner of the Han dynasty, called a "hill censer."
PUNCH'ONG WARE	(Korean) This is a stoneware made of grayish clay in which the surface is covered either partially or wholly with a coating of brushed white slip before the glaze is applied. Often the object is incised and the white slip applied to the incisions or the white slip is applied over the whole object and then a pattern carved out.
PYONGP'UNG	(Korean) Folding screens.

RAMMA	Transom partitions.
RIKYU	A shape of lantern named after a famous tea master (see Sen no Rikyu).
ROKA	Hallway.
RONIN	Masterless samurai.
RYOSHIBAKO	Container for writing paper.
RYU	Dragon.
SAGE-JU	Portable food container for picnics.
SAKAMORI	Communal saké party held on special occasions.
SAKAZUKI	Exchanging cups of saké.
SAKÉ	Rice wine.
SAKURA	Cherry blossoms.
SAMURAI	The warrior class in feudal Japan.
SAN	Poetic inscription sometimes found on hanging scrolls.
SANBO	Stands, trays on platforms.
SANGAKU	An early mime and acrobatic entertainment, predecessor of the Noh drama.
SEIDO TORO	Bronze lanterns.
SEN NO RIKYU	A famous tea master considered the father of the modern tea ceremony.
SENSU	Paper folding fan.
SETO	One of the "six ancient kilns" famous for its pottery; later one of the largest porcelain producing areas and still active today.
SHAKU	A sceptor made of wood, a symbol of authority, used by the emperor and high clergy.
SHAKUDO	Metal alloy containing copper and gold.
SHAMISEN	Three-stringed musical instrument used frequently in Japanese kabuki and Noh dramas.
SHIBAI-E	Woodblock prints of famous actors and theatrical scenes.
SHIBARARE JIZO	Patron saint for the return of stolen property.
SHIBUICHI	Metal alloy containing silver and copper.
SHIGA-JIKU	Hanging scroll with poetry inscribed.
SHIGARAKI	One of the "six ancient kilns" famous for its pottery.
SHINTO	The native religion of Japan.
SHIRO-GANE	White metal containing lead and silver.
SHISHI	Mythological animal resembling a lion.
SHITE	Main actor in a Noh drama.

SHO	Calligraphy.
SHODANA	Bookcase.
SHOIN	Reading room or study.
SHOKI-IMARI	The earliest Japanese porcelain produced from around 1600 to 1650.
SHOKUDAI	Candlesticks.
SHOSOIN	The imperial treasurehouse built in the mid eighth century in Nara to hold the belongings of the Emperor Shomu. It houses some of the oldest examples of Chinese and Japanese artifacts in existence.
SHUNGA	Woodblock prints depicting erotic scenes.
SOBA	Buckwheat noodles.
SOBA-CHOKO	Cups for holding the sauce served with Japanese noodles.
SOBA-YA	Noodle restaurant.
SOKU	Bolsters used as armrests when seated on *tatami* mats.
SUIBOKU	Black ink painting.
SUITEKI	Containers used for water to soften the ink stick in *sumi* painting.
SUMI	Black ink.
SUMI-E	Black ink paintings.
SUMI-TSUBO	Carpenter's tool used to mark a straight line.
SUMO-E	Woodblock prints showing scenes from sumo and depicting famous sumo wrestlers.
SUZURI	Inkstone.
SUZURI-BAKO	Writing, or inkstone box.
TABAKO-BON	Smoking boxes or trays.
TAKAMAKI-E	Low relief lacquer decoration.
TAMBA	One of the "six ancient kilns" famous for its pottery.
TANSU	Wooden chests.
TARAI	Basin used to hold water for personal grooming.
TATAMI	Straw mat flooring used in the traditional Japanese house or building.
TE-ABURI HIBACHI	Handwarming brazier.
TEBAKO	Cosmetic boxes, literally "hand box."
TEMMYO-GAMA	Iron kettles for the tea ceremony featuring rough surfaces.
TENUGUI KAKE	Towel rack.
TESSEN	Iron folding fan used by warriors.
TETSUBIN	Iron or porcelain tea kettle.

TING	Ancient Chinese ceremonial bronze shape, a cauldron with three legs.
TODAI	Candle stand or dish.
TOFU	Bean curd, a protein-rich, common Japanese food that comes in a variety of forms.
TOKONAME	One of the "six ancient kilns" famous for its pottery.
TOKONOMA	Display alcove in a Japanese room.
TOSA	A Japanese school of painting that dealt with literary subjects from the classics in a refined manner.
TOSHIKOSHI-SOBA	"Year crossing" noodles eaten on New Year's Eve.
TSUBA	Sword guard.
TSUNO-DARAI	Horn-handled basin.
TSURU	Crane.
UGUISU NO FUN	Japanese nightingale droppings popular as a skin treatment among women.
UKIYO-E	Woodblock prints associated with the colorful "floating world" of old Edo (Tokyo) during the 17th, 18th, and early 19th centuries.
URUSHI	Lacquer.
UTA-KAI	Literally "song shell," a game of matching shells on which poetry is written.
WAGON	Six-stringed cithern, one of the oldest native Japanese musical instruments.
WARIBASHI	Split chopsticks carried as part of the sword equipment.
YAMATO	The old Japanese heartland area, now Nara Prefecture.
YAMATO-BUE	A six-holed, bamboo flute native to Japan.
YAMATO-E	A native Japanese style of painting.
YOKOHAMA-E	Woodblock prints depicting foreigners.
YOKOZUNA	In sumo wrestling, the highest rank of "grand champion."
YOME-IRI-DANSU	Bridal chest.
YUKATA	A summer robe made of cotton with patterns dyed in blue and white.
YUTANPO	A hot water bottle made of metal or porcelain.
YUTO	Hot water pitcher.
ZEN	Serving trays.
ZENGA	Pictorial expressions of Zen Buddhism.
ZENI-BAKO	Money boxes.
ZENI-DANSU	Money storage chests.

INDEX

PHOTO CREDITS